How to be Inventive When Teaching Primary Mathematics

Have you ever taken your children on a maths walk?
Are your pupils shape detectives?

How to be Inventive When Teaching Primary Mathematics is a pocket guide to inspire primary teachers to become confident, effective, imaginative teachers who enjoy teaching and whose pupils enjoy learning. It is packed with exciting, creative, unexpected ideas to help teachers and pupils open their eyes to the mathematical world around them. It gives teachers the tools to develop their own classroom activities and experiences, supporting learners as they move fluently between mathematical ideas and develop their ownership of mathematics: take your pupils on a maths walk, meet dinosaurs, visit art galleries, learn your destiny number, create your first human graph in the playground and learn how to be an algebra magician.

Written by Steve Humble, expert teacher, teacher trainer and, as Dr Maths, advocate for the power and potential of mathematics, this friendly, stimulating guide offers a fresh, practical approach to teaching mathematics based on the best research and practice, and years of experience in the field. Focussing on five key mathematical topics – number, geometry, measurement, statistics and algebra – it is structured in the form of a journey, introducing historical facts, ideas for innovative and inventive classroom activities and explorations of the key misconceptions for each topic.

How to be Inventive When Teaching Primary Mathematics will challenge you to think about your own beliefs and how they influence your practice, and help you understand how best to transform your teaching to stimulate children's emotions to improve knowledge, learning and enjoyment of the beauty of maths.

Steve Humble is Teaching Fellow for secondary and primary PGCE mathematics at Newcastle University, UK. In his role as a maths publicist – Dr Maths – Steve writes books, blogs and a fortnightly newspaper column to help create greater public interest and understanding of mathematics.

How to be Inventive When Teaching Primary Mathematics

Developing outstanding learners

Steve Humble

Routledge
Taylor & Francis Group

LONDON AND NEW YORK

First published 2015
by Routledge
2 Park Square, Milton Park, Abingdon, Oxon OX14 4RN

and by Routledge
711 Third Avenue, New York, NY 10017

Routledge is an imprint of the Taylor & Francis Group, an informa business

British Library Cataloguing in Publication Data
A catalogue record for this book is available from the British Library

Library of Congress Cataloging in Publication Data
How to be inventive when teaching primary mathematics: developing
outstanding learners/Steve Humble.
    pages cm
    1. Mathematics – Study and teaching (Elementary). 2. Elementary
    school teachers – Training of. 3. Mathematics teachers – Training of.
    I. Title.
    QA135.6.H855 2015
    372.7 – dc23
    2014038953

ISBN: 978-1-138-84341-7 (hbk)
ISBN: 978-1-138-84342-4 (pbk)
ISBN: 978-1-315-73101-8 (ebk)

Typeset in Celeste and Optima
by Florence Production Ltd, Stoodleigh, Devon, UK

Printed and bound in the United States of America by Publishers Graphics,
LLC on sustainably sourced paper.

Paws, this book is for you.

Thank you

Contents

List of illustrations   ix
About the author   xii

Introduction   1

1 Our mathematical world   4

2 Starting points: number   17

3 More and more numbers   36

4 On the journey: measurement   53

5 Many paths to take: geometry   67

6 Ownership: statistics and probability   80

7 Almost there: algebra   93

8 Starting your own new journey   108

Appendix   115
Glossary   130
References   136
Index   139

Illustrations

FIGURES

1.1	Cauliflower fractals	5
2.1	Babylonian numerals	18
2.2	Egyptian and Chinese numbers	19
2.3	Pythagoras	20
2.4	Celebrity destiny numbers	22
2.5	Pocket money puzzle and average distance from the Earth to the Moon	27
2.6	House numbers	30
2.7	Playground game markings	32
2.8	Triangular numbers	33
2.9	Visual illustrations of 12 as 3×4 and 15 as 5×3	35
3.1	The Eye of Horus	37
3.2	Dividing a shape into two	39
3.3	Equivalent fraction cards	40
3.4	Visual representation of a half	41
3.5	Visual representation of a third	41
3.6	Overlapping grid for addition of fractions	42
3.7	Addition using visual methods	42
3.8	Visual method to calculate $\frac{1}{3} + \frac{2}{5}$	43
3.9	Venn diagram showing the set of all real numbers	45
3.10	Examples of a Venn diagram	45
3.11	Repeated subtraction	50
4.1	Dinosaur footprint	57

4.2 Carrots from Mr McGregor's garden   58
4.3 Clocks   59
4.4 Historical timeline   61
4.5 Analemmatic sundial   62
4.6 Chinese zodiac   64
4.7 Lunar phases   65
5.1 Platonic solids   68
5.2 'Quarry' by Paul Klee   70
5.3 Andy Goldsworthy's art   71
5.4 Net of a cube   74
5.5 Tessellations and art   75
5.6 Regular two-dimensional tessellated polygons   75
5.7 The 12 possible hexiamonds   76
5.8 Hexiamond pictures   77
5.9 Alphabet symmetry   78
5.10 Pentagons   79
6.1 Abraham de Moivre   81
6.2 Halfway down the stairs   83
6.3 Temperature gauge   86
6.4 Probability scale   88
7.1 Everyday symbols   95
7.2 $x + 6 = 10$ 96
7.3 $x + x + 7 = 25 - x$ or $2x + 7 = 25 - x$ 96
7.4 $y + x = 5$ 97
7.5 Leonhard Euler   105
7.6 Cube   106
8.1 Memory and the adaptive role in the response to future situations   112
A.1 Benford's Law   116
A.2 Patterns in the primes   117
A.3 The golden ratio   118
A.4 Triangle pattern with ten start   121
A.5 Triangle patterns with four start   122
A.6 Three-line triangle   128
A.7 Four-, five- and six-line triangles   128
A.8 Kobon triangle puzzle   128

TABLES

2.1	Destiny number interpretation	22
2.2	Digital root	26
3.1	Carbon footprint calculator	50
3.2	Carbon emissions by transport	51
5.1	Mirror code	78
6.1	Probability for throwing two coins	89
7.1	Think of a number – No. 1	99
7.2	Think of a number – No. 1 – answer	100
7.3	Think of a number – No. 2 – answer	100
7.4	Pick a card	101
7.5	Pick a card algebra	102
7.6	The consequences game	104
7.7	Shapes and Euler's formula	106
A.1	Persistence table	123
A.2	Kobon triangle	129

About the author

With over 20 years experience as a mathematics subject leader in various educational establishments, I became the Senior Regional Coordinator for the National Centre for Excellence in the Teaching of Mathematics (NCETM), which I undertook for five years. Currently I work at Newcastle University, teaching mathematics on the primary and secondary PGCE. My research focuses on talented children in low-income areas of Dar Es Salaam, Tanzania and their possible contribution to the eradication of poverty. I am also interested in looking at teacher effectiveness in different school management types in India and Africa.

I am a Member of the European Mathematical Society (EMS) Committee for Raising the Public Awareness of Mathematics in Europe and a fellow of the Institute of Mathematics and its Applications (IMA). To promote public interest in mathematics I have written a fortnightly newspaper column as 'Dr Maths', as well as a range of puzzles, 'explorer' books and a number of classroom resources.

My hope is that you see the value in this book and feel you can make it part of your teaching and learning. I welcome your comments and questions.

email: steve.humble@ncl.ac.uk

Look again and see what's new.
Look around and take in the view.
Look again and see what's new.
Human architecture
structures our life.
Designs forged
through centuries might.
The clock ticks on with time underplayed,
sequencing
layers on layers,
that drift and fade.
The walk we take has twists and turns,
patterns only viewed in diminishing returns.
Take some time to think.
Pause.
Take in the view.
Look again.
And see.
What's new?

by Steve Humble (2015)

Introduction

'The time has come,' the Walrus said, 'to talk of many things.'
Lewis Carroll

This book takes a fresh practical look at teaching mathematics. I base this approach not only on my own teaching experience over the past 29 years but also my involvement with teacher continual professional development within and outside university. I have taught maths to many trainee primary school teachers. They often conveyed to me their worries, fears and concerns regarding teaching maths to young children. However, I have always found that with a little bit of confidence, know-how and originality maths teaching can be the most rewarding experience.

The book contains inventive ideas concerning mathematical topics that you will need for teaching in a primary school. These ideas will give you an insight into delivering lessons that show the beauty and power of mathematics. It will allow children to gain a sense of enjoyment and curiosity about the subject.

One sees five topics in the curriculum that you as a primary school teacher need to embrace and transfer to your children: number, geometry, measurement, statistics and algebra. These provide the foundations of mathematical learning.

Looking at this list someone might say: 'I didn't like doing those at school.'

So how can we stop your pupils growing up and saying the same thing? We want them and you to leave school at the end of the day saying 'I want to do more maths at home tonight'. So that's where we'll start.

This guide provides you with some of the tools you will need to teach your pupils in an inventive way. Not only will you inform and stimulate, but you will use methods and ideas that twist and turn to make for some fun, provide original experiences and allow children to move fluently between mathematical ideas.

This book is structured in the form of a journey. You will see within each chapter an historical introduction, followed by ideas around innovative and inventive classroom activities and finishing by exploring the key misconception[1] for that topic.

The book has eight chapters. In Chapter 1 we will take a look around our exciting mathematical world. And yes it is. Once you have worked through this chapter along with your students you'll never look at the world in the same way again. You'll need to switch on your mathematical eyes to see the beauty of maths that exists all around you.

The following six chapters are dedicated to the key themes in primary mathematics school teaching. Irrespective of their inclusion by government these five areas provide building blocks to solve intriguing problems. They provide a foundation that will give children the tools to undertake their continued mathematical development.

Chapter 8 provides some research findings to help you think more about your own beliefs regarding the teaching of mathematics. This includes how some preconceived ideas can affect the way we order and structure our lessons. In this chapter I will consider what research shows regarding beliefs and how we can all benefit from having a wider perspective. To end the book there is an Appendix containing several additional snippets to help you on your way. These include ten 'starting points', which provide ideas for you to develop into lessons and practice your skills. A very short glossary is also included to provide some helpful words that may possibly expand your mathematical vocabulary. This final part of the journey brings the book to a close. But the final part is only just the beginning. You will now be on your own exciting journey. The guide provides you with the knowledge to expand your own teaching methods, practice and expertise. So let's begin to open your mathematical eyes.

NOTE

1 Ryan and Williams (2007) give more detailed research on errors and misconceptions.

Chapter 1

Our mathematical world

If you can count your money, you don't have a billion dollars.

J. Paul Getty

Opening your mathematical eyes in any town, city, village or countryside will allow you (and your students) to experience maths in a new way. Realizing that maths is not just a subject in school but is part of your everyday world gives you more ownership of that knowledge and allows you to see connections that otherwise you may never have associated with maths.

So what do I mean?

Look at the patterns of fields, hedges and lines of trees. How about street grid systems, bridges, buildings and paving stone patterns? Looking more closely at buildings we can often see lines of symmetry in windows, fire escapes and doorways.

Typically our surroundings have been constructed by our ancestors. They were using their logical minds following clear patterns that we can all 'see' but maybe never have.

Until now.

Around us are shapes such as triangles, rectangles and circles, as well as three-dimensional objects such as cuboids, pyramids and spheres. What is interesting is that these shapes are known as Euclidean shapes. They are named after a Greek mathematician, Euclid, who in about 300 BC wrote a series of books which classified all the geometrical properties of different shapes. Euclid created a blueprint that all mathematical architects have used ever since in the construction of the man-made world we live in. Not only may you find this interesting but so will your students.

So tell them.

The reason for telling them is that some of your pupils will be interested in history, people and the past, and maybe not so interested in maths (yes really). Talking about history in your maths lesson will offer a hook upon which to hang mathematics and draw in those students. Ownership of mathematics is also very important for children and adults so they can say: 'this is my maths'. In art and English lessons it's easy for children to have ownership: 'this is my piece of art' or 'these are my thoughts in this essay'. It seems at first glance that in mathematics this is harder to do, if not impossible. I'm going

FIGURE 1.1 Cauliflower fractals

to show you in this book that this is not true and children can have ownership of 'their maths'.

The natural world follows a different blueprint that mathematicians have recently discovered. One such mathematician was Benoit Mandelbrot who wrote a famous book called *The Fractal Geometry of Nature (1983)*. This world he discovered (along with other mathematicians) also has beautiful mathematical symmetries. The geometry of the natural world we now call 'fractals' and can be seen clearly in objects such as ferns and cauliflowers. If you take a part of a fern it looks like the whole fern; likewise each individual floret of a cauliflower looks like the whole cauliflower (Figure 1.1). This is called self-symmetry.

So why not take your class out for a mathematical walk in order to open your children's mathematical eyes? What could be more exciting? It's like a mathematical treasure hunt. The treasures are hidden all around us.

HOW TO PLAN AND ORGANIZE YOUR FIRST MATHS WALK

One way to open your students' mathematical eyes is to take them on a maths walk.

Outdoor maths walks can supply further evidence of enhanced learning. They are meaningful, stimulating, challenging and exciting for children. Most important, these walks invite *all* students, irrespective of their classroom achievement level, to participate successfully in problem solving activities and gain a sense of pride in the mathematics they create. As youngsters discover real-world shapes, patterns, numbers, data, symmetry and reflections – to name just a few examples – their eyes open to the mathematics in their world. They become maths detectives – posing questions and solving problems as well as documenting and communicating their discoveries in multiple ways.

Teachers and parents value insights into children's mathematical learning and the different ways that this learning can be fostered in the home, the local community and the school environment. Adults also appreciate seeing their youngsters totally immersed in learning. As one teacher said during a maths walk I was organizing, 'I've seen my children ready to "pop" because they have been so excited about what they've discovered'.

A typical walk consists of a sequence of designated sites along a planned route where students stop to explore maths in the environment. Maths walks make mathematics come alive for children by engaging them cognitively, physically and emotionally.

First you need to think about what you want your students to see with their mathematical eyes. Plan this beforehand. Go for a walk at the weekend. See if you can find, for example, some fractal symmetry in nature and also some man-made symmetries.

Students and teachers alike can create walks that target a range of mathematical understanding. We can classify maths walks under four main categories:

- **Student-created** – Pupils from the same grade can design a walk for each other. Alternatively older children in the school can create a walk for their younger peers.
- **Teacher-created** – You yourself design the walk. Once the children have had an opportunity to answer the questions along the way you can encourage them to modify your walk to produce a new and improved version.
- **Teacher-created and community** – You not only design the walk for the children but now you include their families as well. These types of walks can explore the school surroundings, their homes and their local community environment.
- **Teacher-created and peers** – Now you have become an expert you can inspire the rest of your colleagues to try a maths walk for themselves. This will allow them to think about mathematics from a different standpoint

involving the use of other subjects such as history and literature, something up until now they may not have considered.

When first creating a maths walk give some initial thought to its proposed purpose and the anticipated learning outcomes. For example, if children are undertaking a unit on shape and pattern, then the maths walk could focus on exploring various shape and pattern examples in the school buildings and in the grounds, e.g. let them become 'shape detectives'.

Here are some useful starting questions upon which to base your initial discussion with the class:

- Find three objects where you can see one line of symmetry.
- Find an object with rotational symmetry.
- Find a repeating pattern.
- Find an object that is approximately one metre tall.

Alternatively, the maths walk's purpose could be to introduce students to where mathematics can be found in our everyday world. These can include locations that have scientific, historical, literary, engineering or business significance. To this end students could examine the structure of a nearby bridge, explore the brick or tile designs on a local historical building, or investigate science museum displays.

HOW TO STRUCTURE YOUR CLASS FOR THEIR VERY FIRST MATHS WALK

Introduce children to maths walks by having them explore, in small groups, four or five areas of interest within their own classroom (e.g. the reading corner, the science project display). At each area of interest, have groups respond to one or two questions such as these:

1. In which ways could we find out about books that are the most popular in our class?
2. How might you rearrange the bookshelves so we can add more books?

Alternatively you could initiate the process by getting children to think about how a specific mathematical concept could be present in their everyday world. For example you may ask a specific question, such as: how many different ways can you find the number 5?

Here are some ideas to help start your discussion:

*   Find 5 different colours in the classroom.
*   Find or write a story involving the number 5.
*   Name 5 different breakfast cereals you have eaten.
*   Which are your 5 favourite toys?
*   Find 5 different shapes in the classroom.
*   What did you do yesterday afternoon at 5 o'clock?
*   What time will it be in 5 minutes?
*   What is the shortest and longest distance you can travel in 5 steps?
*   If you walk through 5 doors, where will you be?

Now that the children have had time to experience developing mathematical questions of their own, and to follow up with a class discussion, you can take things further.

Say to your class: 'look at that. Look around you.' Then ask some starting point questions to help them switch on their mathematical eyes:

*   What can you see?
*   How many?
*   How far or near?
*   How long, short, tall, high, deep, heavy?
*   How many lines? How sharp? How curved?
*   How many objects in a line? How many in a shape?

- How much do you see? How much more is hidden?
- Can you find 5 of these . . .? Estimate the size, height, length, weight of . . .
- What is the name of . . .?
- What kind of number?
- What kind of pattern? Can you continue this pattern?
- What kind of shape?
- What shapes do you see? Draw them.
- Name some of the shapes you have found. Did you find the . . .?
- Why do you think lots of triangles have been used to . . .?
- Why do you think the bridge is arched?
- Why do you think the path does not follow a straight line?
- What if we change this?
- What if we add a line? What if we add a shape?
- What difference does it make? Is it still symmetrical?
- What if we double it?
- What if we change the area?
- What if we alter the symmetry?
- Could you make a pattern with . . .? Show that this works.
- Is it always true?

You might like to take a pause from reading for a minute or two and look around the space you are sitting in. How many different mathematical questions can you make?

Now you and your children have the idea of constructing mathematical questions from the environment around you it could be the time to take them outside of the classroom.

First of all you will need to create eight numbered locations in the playground and assign teams of children to each location. When outside you could use the school's playground markings as some of these locations. As children observe these areas of interest, have them develop questions that they would like their peers to answer. To keep things fresh and interesting you should move them to their next location after having five minutes of question writing time. For a student-generated maths walk, which is what you are instigating here, you will need to devote 45 to 60 minutes to small-group exploration of places and objects of mathematical interest outside the classroom.

A worthwhile component of outside learning is to assign a data crew to document the responses of each group at each site location. A data crew comprises two to three children whose task is to collect pertinent data such as digital photographs, brief video recordings and the groups' written responses.

On your return to the classroom, give students opportunities to share their maths walk discoveries and solutions to problems. As the basis of a whole-class discussion on the outcome of the math's walk, the data crew could initially report on what they collected and observed. The various documented accounts of the children's responses are important when students share and assess questions around the eight locations. You can be as inventive as you like and could include the data crew's photographs and video records.

Have groups share their questions with the entire class and decide which ones are the 'best' and 'most appropriate' to use as a basis for making a maths walk. The children should justify their selection focusing on the mathematical appeal, diversity and challenge of the questions and problems. In order to help them on their way you could ask them to:

- **compare** problem solutions and how they were generated;
- **report** any difficulties, challenges and additional questions that arose in exploring each site;
- **share** ways to improve the maths walk.

As students work on their maths walk, teachers can gain important insights into their mathematical understanding or lack thereof. When looking at shape I have come across an instance where children did not understand the properties of a square, something that would not have been raised in class, as presumptions around knowledge and understanding are less explored or vocalized. In such an informal environment with the children working in groups and as peers, instigate honest discussion about uncertainties and misunderstandings around mathematical concepts.

CONCEPTUAL UNDERSTANDING

Children's maths walk experiences can serve as 'transfer triggers'.

One example of this could be when students investigate symmetry: you could remind them of when they used their mathematical eyes on their outdoor maths walk. For example, they might have looked at the doors and windows of the school building. You might even revisit the site to refresh their memories about symmetrical patterns.

These memories of the outdoor world are very strong and form the basis to build further learning about mathematical concepts. This notion of building mathematical learning from existing real-life memories promotes transfer triggers and stronger long-term connections with mathematical concepts.

When assessing children's learning during and after the maths walk, you might like to consider that:

- there are **different** ways in which individual students solved the maths walk problems;
- there are **interactions** with their peers in solving the problems;
- there are **conceptual** strengths and limitations evident in each child's responses and interactions;
- there is a **core** mathematical content that has been revealed by the maths walk as needing further development, explanation or to be given more understanding in the classroom.

Maths walks empower lifelong learning. Integrating 'outside' mathematics with 'inside' classroom mathematics can sow the seeds for developing flexible, creative, future-oriented mathematical thinkers and problem solvers.

EXAMPLES OF MATHS WALKS

Here are a few questions from different types of maths walks, to give you some ideas on how to create your own.

Example 1

These first questions come from a class of seven year olds I was working with who were creating an Easter maths walk for a parent–child activity day.

The activity day gives parents an opportunity to observe their children's mathematical learning and to allow them to appreciate that such learning does not always need to take place within a classroom. This endeavour was designed to promote future family journeys involving greater awareness of maths in the community.

Here are two questions that the children devised for their walk:

(1) What shapes can you see in the railings over the bridge? Circle the types of shapes you can see using the diagram below. Can you find any other shapes? Draw them in the space.

(2) Starting at one pair of benches find a route to the other pair of benches.

During your journey from one pair of benches to the other you need to run around each piece of the playground equipment once and only once.

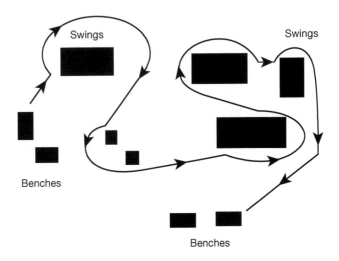

Example 2

I initially created the 'Newcastle and Gateshead' Quayside maths walk with the help of some local teachers, using questions which involved spatial patterns, spatial reasoning, measurement, number, data collection and analysis.

The teachers then presented the maths walk to four classes of 9 to 11 year olds, who worked for two one-hour workshop periods to improve the teacher-generated trail. In groups they explored the walk and reflected on the questions and problems the teachers had created.

Back in class, the children discussed and justified which questions and problems they considered the most appealing and worthwhile and then suggested changes.

Here are some of the questions that passed the students' inspection:

1(a) Check the timetable, and find the times for the first and last bus on Friday.

1(b) On Friday how many hours and minutes out of a 24-hour day do the buses not run?

2(a) Make an imaginary line between you and the road across the River Tyne. Working in pairs for three minutes, complete the tally chart below to record the number of vehicles that cross over your imaginary line.

Boats	
Buses	
Cars	
Vans	
Cyclists	

2(b) From the data you have collected estimate the number of vans that would cross your line in an hour.

Example 3

To celebrate 150 years of the London Underground I was asked to create a general maths walk that could be used at any of the 270 Tube stations. Here are a few of those questions from the 'Labyrinth family Tube walk':

(1) Perfect patterns – Design has always played a big part in the London Underground. Look around you – up, down, left and right. What patterns can you see?
Look at the walls, floors, stairs and entrances of stations. Notice patterns on and within Tube carriages.
Describe or draw three of the different patterns you can see on the Underground in the box below and note where you saw them.

(2) Number cruncher – Each Underground train carriage has an identification number. These numbers can be

three, four or five digits long. Similarly, each labyrinth artwork is numbered at the bottom right-hand corner.

Your challenge is to make a calculation equalling the labyrinth number using only the digits of your train carriage number.

For example, if your carriage number is 5,547 and the labyrinth number is 22 then you could create the following calculation: $4 \times 5 + 7 - 5 = 22$

If your carriage number is 21,060 and the labyrinth number is 63 then you could create either one of the following calculations:

$$60 + 2 + 1 \text{ or } 2^6 - 1 = 2 \times 2 \times 2 \times 2 \times 2 \times 2 - 1$$

CONCLUSION

This chapter has encouraged you and your students to open their mathematical eyes by taking a journey outside. Curiosity about the world around us as well as through other subject ideas can all help to stimulate children to want to engage with maths.

Hopefully you can now see that maths appears everywhere and it's exciting to use with your students. We now move forward on our journey. Our second starting point is 'number', where mathematics all began.

Chapter 2

Starting points
Number

> Not everything that counts can be counted,
> and not everything that can be counted counts.
>
> Albert Einstein

The next six chapters all use the same structure, that is through engaging activities you will be reminded of the maths you learnt at school and be given very practical ideas of how you can teach each topic in perhaps a more engaging, enriching and inventive way.

This chapter looks at whole numbers that provide the building blocks of mathematics. I start by providing you with a brief look at the origins of number, which you may want to relate to your students. This is followed by a selection of classroom activities that are all designed to motivate children's curiosity about number. The activities approach 'number' using different starting points to act as hooks to draw in children with different interests and learning styles.

HISTORICAL BACKGROUND

It is believed that counting first began when we were hunter-gatherers. This is before we started to divide the land into regular rectangular patches as farmers. To hunters there was only a need for 'one', 'two' and 'many', as they could only hold two objects at once. The use of other numbers was relatively irrelevant. Therefore after 'two' came 'many'.

When we settled down and started to farm, the land was divided up into areas for domesticated animals on which they could graze. The farmer needed to keep an inventory of his animals and thus there was a need to have the ability to count. You can imagine the scene. The farmer is in the initial stages of deciding what base unit to use and how to record totals. It is only lucky that the farmer had all of his fingers or we could be counting in base eight! We have ten fingers, so this was an obvious unit to start counting in. But what do you do if you have more than ten sheep? Well, again the farmer would have looked around and found something suitable within his environment exploring (unbeknown to him) with his mathematical eyes. He therefore could have used stones or pebbles for counting his tens and possibly larger stones for hundreds. This is how we believe our 'base ten' number system was developed; first by the Babylonians (Figure 2.1) and subsequently evolving into our present-day Arabic numerals, zero to nine.

There are interesting historical stories that you can discuss or relate to your children concerning the development of number

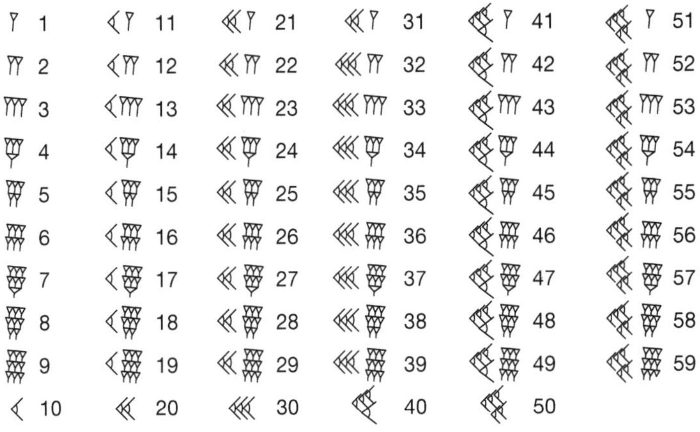

FIGURE 2.1 Babylonian numerals

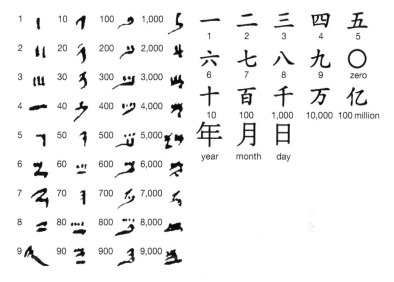

FIGURE 2.2 Egyptian and Chinese numbers

patterns in different cultures and countries. Using mathematical history alongside interesting stories and facts will intrigue some students and engage their learning.

Mathematicians have been fascinated by number patterns from the beginning. The Egyptians recorded numbers in rows of three strokes. The Chinese recorded numbers as horizontal bars with a pattern layout, as seen in Figure 2.2.

CLASSROOM ACTIVITIES: WHOLE NUMBERS

Destiny number

You will probably remember Pythagoras from school. The sixth-century BC Greek is one of the few, if not the only, mathematician that is ever mentioned in secondary school classes. He is remembered today for his rule connecting the sides of a right-angled triangle.

Ask any adult what they remember of Pythagoras and they will say something like 'it's the square on the hippopotamus

FIGURE 2.3 Pythagoras

side that's worth two of something else'. We could say that's almost right for learning something more than likely by rote with no link to your real world experiences. In fact what Pythagoras's theorem states is that:

'The square on the hypotenuse equals the sum of the squares on the other two sides'.

History tells us that Pythagoras entertained large audiences with stories about the qualities he applied to numbers in terms of 'numerology' and the mathematical patterns and relationships he had developed. Before we look at more standard number patterns let us digress into the world of Pythagoras. He was obsessed with whole numbers and their beauty. There is a story that goes something like this.

Pythagoras was sitting happily in his office working on his beautiful whole numbers when in pops one of his disciples, Hippasus. He is very happy and could not hold back his excitement.

'Pythagoras, Pythagoras, look! The square root of 2 cannot be written as a fraction. What do you think? Amazing isn't it?'

But Pythagoras was not amazed, he was very angry. In fact he was really angry and said to Hippasus that he had blasphemed against the beauty of numbers and that he would have to be drowned as an example to others not to slur numbers in this way.

As you will understand from reading this short story about Pythagoras he lived in a very different world, but if you tell this story to your class they will be intrigued and want to find out more about this man and his numbers.

Pythagoras had an obsession with whole numbers, as you will have guessed from the story. Out of this obsession developed the science of numerology, the belief that whole numbers can somehow predict your destiny. In his theory one's date of birth can be used to determine one's romantic penchants.

He called this your 'destiny number'. He thought that by revealing the simple truths of the numbers 1 to 9, individuals would be able to know themselves better.

So have I grabbed your attention?

Do you want to know your very own romantic destiny number?

You can do this by adding the numbers in your birth date. Let's look at a couple of examples. Albert Einstein was born on 14 March 1879. The calculation for his destiny number would be $1 + 4 + 3 + 1 + 8 + 7 + 9$; that is the 14th day of the 3rd month in 1879. These numbers give a total of 33. You then need to add the digits in this number, and keep adding them if necessary, until you get a single figure. In the case of Albert Einstein this gives 6 ($3 + 3$). Keep this number in mind as we'll find out how romantic Albert was in his day according to Pythagoras after we've looked at another celebrity.

How about the film and fashion icon Audrey Hepburn?

She was born on 4 May 1929. This date of birth gives a score of $4 + 5 + 1 + 9 + 2 + 9$, which adds up to 30. Then adding the digits $3 + 0$ to finish up with a single digit we have the answer 3.

21

FIGURE 2.4

Celebrity destiny numbers: Albert Einstein (junior wannabe in your class) and Audrey Hepburn

So here's what you've been waiting for. What do these numbers mean in terms of romance? For Albert Einstein, with a destiny number of 6 this, implies he is 'romantic and enjoys making others feel special'. Audrey on the other hand as a 3 was 'adventurous, loved fun and going out'.

TABLE 2.1 Destiny number interpretation

1	Free spirited – outgoing nature
2	Easy going – no hassles for you
3	Adventurous – love fun and going out
4	Disciplined – work hard at relationships
5	Mischievous – active and bubbly
6	Romantic – enjoy making others feel special
7	Instinctive – full of common sense
8	Charming – confident and attractive
9	Generous – always wanting to help

So what are you?

I probably didn't need to write that last sentence. I guess you had already started to work out your own destiny number. Am I right?

I captured your interest and motivated you to do some mathematics. That's what you want to do with your class.

This engaging technique is called 'episodic learning'. We have created a moment in the child's mind. They have a memory – an episode. On to this memory we are going to build learning. Research shows (I'll talk more about this in Chapter 8) that these types of learning moments can help to develop stronger and more long lasting memories, which help cultivate learning.

Your question might be: how do I use this initial historical starter and activity to feed into the rest of the lesson?

In calculating the numerology number you had to do a calculation that involved working out something mathematicians call 'digital roots'. Numerologists are not alone in using digital roots. Magicians also use them. Therefore we can use 'magic maths' to continue our lesson on basic number work. Using the hook of magic will engage other children in your class to be motivated to do lots of calculations.

All children need to learn how to add and subtract whole numbers. By using the hook of magic you are making this maths lesson meaningful and fun. Children are more likely to go home that evening and try some mathematics with their parents, showing them the 'trick'. In a way it is not about the magic. It's about using it as a vehicle to engage children in the activity of calculation and enjoying number. So here's an example.

Abracadabra: magic maths

As a teacher you are many things. According to the educationalist Michael Marland, in order to be able to carry out the 'craft' of teaching one is required at different times to play the parts of 'the salesman, the music hall performer, the parent, the clown, the intellectual, the lover and the organiser'.[1]

23

For this activity you are going to play the part of a magician. Your classroom is a theatre and your students are the spectators.

As the magician you ask a spectator (one of your pupils) to write down any three-digit number.[2] Then ask to see this number. In 'secret' you will then make a prediction (as set out below) about the final single number, which will be revealed at the end of the trick. You can write your prediction on a piece of paper and ask one of the spectators to look after it for you and keep it safe.

For example, if the spectator had chosen 538, the magician would secretly add $5 + 3 + 8$ to get 16, then $1 + 6$ to get 7. Hence, using the same technique as Pythagoras in his destiny numbers (digital root), the number 7 is secretly written on a piece of paper.

The magician then asks the same spectator to write down five or more numbers, which when added together give the initial three-digit number (in this example 538).

In order to involve the whole class ask all the children to write down any five numbers that add up to 538. There are many options, but one example could be that a spectator would write down $400 + 112 + 16 + 7 + 3$. The magician then asks the spectators to add up the digits in these numbers. In the example above this would be $4 + 0 + 0 + 1 + 1 + 2 + 1 + 6 + 7 + 3 = 25$. As in the destiny numbers we need to continue doing this until we end up with a single digit: hence $2 + 5 = 7$.

The magician (you) then reveals his or her prediction from the start of the trick, which matches the spectator's answer: 7.

The strange thing is, however, that any addition sum of 538 will always give 7, if you keep adding up the digits until you end up with a single digit.

Try it for yourself, with any number.

You can ask the class to try this trick as the magician and spectator in pairs. They could also think about how they could be more creative and deliver their trick to the whole class. One way you could suggest to the class of being inventive is to generate the initial number in different ways, such as:

- Throwing a dice three times, the first throw for the hundreds, the second throw for the tens and the third throw for the units.
- Using a pack of cards (ace to nine) and selecting three at random to gain the three digits of the number (again hundreds, tens, units).

There are many different number magic tricks, which can be explored by children, using digital roots. In the example above the children were practising their addition, so now let's look at how to use a very similar magic trick to inspire a lesson in the subtraction of whole numbers.

Set the scene in the same way as in the example above. You are the magician and you ask a spectator (pupil) to write down a three-digit number without letting you see.

The magician then asks the spectator to write down these digits in a different order and perform a subtraction sum, taking away the smaller of the two numbers from the largest.

For example, if they write down 356, the spectator may write down 563 and do the subtraction sum 563 − 356 = 207.

The magician then asks the spectator to tell him out loud any two of the digits from the answer and then predicts the hidden third digit.

The magician does this by adding the numbers given, and calculating the required value to make this total up to a multiple of 9. For example, if given 0 and 7, the total is 7 and the difference required to make the total up to 9 is 2. Therefore the answer is 2.

When performing this trick it is best to say that the hidden number must be a digit from 1 to 8, as this will avoid the problem of not knowing whether the unknown digit is 0 or 9. Although if you want to live dangerously you can leave these numbers in, and when the total is a multiple of 9 say 'nothing comes to mind'. Then look for the spectator's reaction. If it's positive, then 0 is their number and you will have it right. If not they will still be waiting for you to say 'your hidden number is nine'.

So why do both of these number magic tricks work? It is due to the property of the number nine in our number system (digital root).[3] The highest single digit we can have in our base ten system is nine. Because of this the number nine has special properties. Here are some random numbers and their digital roots (538 is there because of the magicians trick!). Can you see any pattern?

TABLE 2.2 Digital root

Number	Addition	Remainder	Digital Root
10	= 9 + 1	1	1 + 0 = 1
11	= 9 + 2	2	1 + 1 = 2
12	= 9 + 3	3	1 + 2 = 3
17	= 9 + 8	8	1 + 7 = 8
18	= 9 + 9	9	1 + 8 = 9
23	= 2 × 9 + 5	5	2 + 3 = 5
156	= 17 × 9 + 3	3	1 + 5 + 6 = 12 1 + 2 = 3
538	= 59 × 9 + 7	7	5 + 3 + 8 = 16 1 + 6 = 7

If you divide each number by 9 and find the remainder you get the digital root. For example $156 \div 9 = 17$ remainder 3. The digital root is 3. However, note that for any number divisible by 9 the digital root is always 9.

We will come back to magic later in the book as I feel with the right connections to learning it offers some students a motivational hook. These sorts of activities can easily be used to develop positive memories of mathematics. As with the 'history starters' it gives you another way of engaging students in the richness of number.

Puzzles: let's look at money (£)

It is essential for children during their mathematical develop-ment to know and understand the patterns in place value and how this links to our base 10 number system. Children need to be able to interpret the value of each of the ten digits (0, 1, 2, 3, 4, 5, 6, 7, 8, 9) according to its position. Place value is not an easy concept for children to grasp and it is best explained with concrete examples. Money is often a useful place to start. Children can typically appreciate that the 8 in 8p is different to the 8 in 80p and 800p. Here is an illustration of how you could start a practical lesson using a puzzle[4] to teach money and place value:

> If you were given pocket money of 1p the first week, then 2p the second week, 4p the third week, 8p the fourth, and so on, doubling up each week, how long would it be before you had saved one million pounds?

> Answer: 27 weeks.

Were you shocked? It seems incredible.

Week 10	£5.12
Week 11	£10.24
Week 12	£20.48
Week 20	£5,242.88
Week 21	£10,485.76
Week 25	£167,772.16
Week 26	£335,544.32
Week 27	£671,088.64

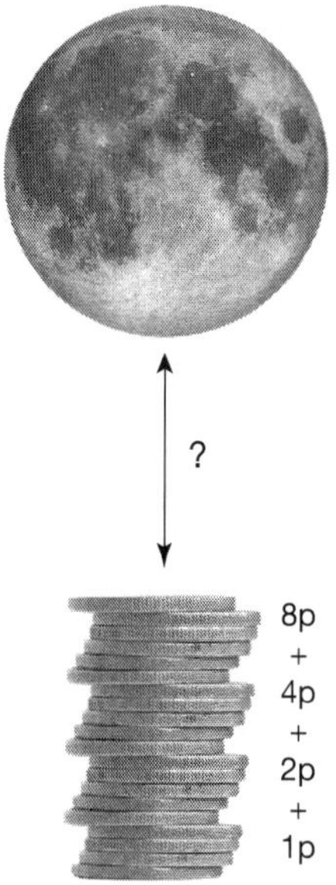

8p
+
4p
+
2p
+
1p

FIGURE 2.5 Pocket money puzzle and average distance from the Earth to the Moon

27

It is one of those problems that has an answer you just cannot believe. Only 27 weeks for you to save up your pocket money and become a millionaire. Amazing!

With the class or just now by yourself, get a pencil and paper and check for yourself. So how does this work? Well when you keep doubling the totals they start to give very big answers. Figure 2.5 provides some of the last few calculations.

Extending the puzzle further ask:

If the average distance from the Earth to the Moon is 384,400 km or 384,400,000,000 mm and a 1p coin has a thickness of about 1.5 mm how many weeks pocket money would it take to make a tower of 1p coins to reach the moon?

It's easy to engage the class with an activity like this. You might bring in a pile of coins to class and make more accurate measurements of the thickness of a coin to get the exact number of coins required.

You have now got the children thinking about very large numbers through sums of money and the idea of how we use place value to represent this. If you want to extend these activities you could pose the following questions for your class to consider:

- How tall in 1p coins is one million pounds?
- How many 1p coins does it take to reach the height of the school?
- How many 1p coins does it take to reach the height of the Empire State Building?
- How many 1p coins does it take to reach the height of Mount Everest?
- How many 10p coins does it take to reach the height of your teacher? How much money is this?

Puzzles are a great way to improve mathematical understanding. It is good for children from a young age to exercise their brains with puzzles. Overall problem-solving ability has been shown by research to improve with mental exercise. Puzzles do just that.

Patterns: odd and even numbers

Chapter 1 highlighted that pattern spotting was important in our outside maths activities. Already in this chapter we have seen how pattern spotting is an underlying concept in number. In fact at all levels of learning mathematics we are trying to spot patterns, from the young child who spots that each time they add 1 they get the next number in the series of whole numbers, to the eminent professor who looks for patterns in data.

Now let's look at some basic number patterns and how you can teach these to your class. One of the simplest patterns is seen in the whole numbers 1, 2, 3, 4, 5, 6, 7, etc.

The pattern starts at 1 and the rule is to add 1 each time. It is always good to use multiple representations when teaching, so show the same number pattern as a number line but also visually by using counters or blocks.

Even numbers form another pattern containing all the numbers in the two times table: 2, 4, 6, 8, 10, 12, etc.

Odd numbers are those not in the two times table: 1, 3, 5, 7, 9, etc.

These numbers are used in real life; for example, in the case of house numbers, on one side of the street they would often be even and on the opposite side odd.

First of all you could ask your class to use their mathematical eyes to look around, thinking about being an 'even and odd number detective'. Once the children have established this concrete relationship with these numbers you can abstract this to look at the properties of the numbers and how they associate with each other.

Some questions for the class to begin this abstraction are:

- When you add two even numbers together do you always get an even number?

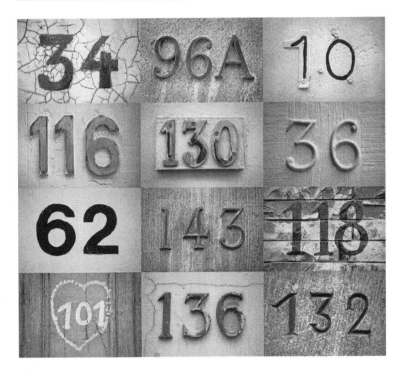

■ **FIGURE 2.6** House numbers

When you add two odd numbers do you always get an even number?

- When you add any two numbers together do you always get an even number?
- What happens when you add three numbers together? Is your answer always even or odd?

Games: number patterns

Using games you can explore the teaching of whole number concepts in a range of different ways. Children with different learning styles in your class will benefit from a variety of game activities. It is important when thinking about your maths lessons that you offer the children in your class these different experiences. The following examples include children using playing cards in pairs, using counters and pebbles to consider odd and even numbers, as well as playing mathematical games in the playground.

Using a pack of cards with the picture cards removed has many possibilities for the learning of number.

Children can work in pairs with a pack of cards. Tell them to shuffle the pack, split the pack between them, so they now have half each. They each turn over a card and play a variation of snap. When two of the cards add up to an even number the children have to call out 'even'. When a player shouts 'even' first, they keep the pair of cards and score one point for that snap. Whoever has the most snaps at the end wins.

When the children become more proficient you can do the same with odd number totals and then try a variation which involves turning over three cards with three players in a group.

A more advanced game for older children combining logic with odd and even numbers is played using counters or pebbles. Two players place 15 pebbles (or counters) between them on the table. Each player takes it in turn to pick up from the pile one, two or three pebbles (it's their choice which). The winner is the one who finishes with an odd number of pebbles in their pile. Once the students have played the game several times and have become familiar with it you can ask them the logic question: is their a strategy the second player can use so they can always win?

In a chapter concerning whole numbers I can't not include prime numbers. A prime number is one which can only be divided by itself and 1 without a remainder. Here is a list of the primes below 100:

2, 3, 5, 7, 11, 13, 17, 19, 23, 29, 31, 37, 41, 43, 47, 53, 59, 61, 67, 71, 73, 79, 83, 89, 97.

Here is an idea for a physical game[5] that your students could play in the playground using odds, evens and primes. One player stands in each of the four numbered squares.

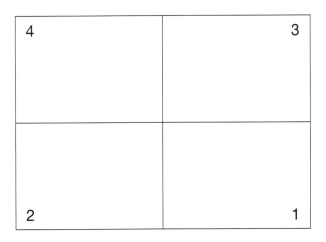

4	3
2	1

FIGURE 2.7 Playground game markings

The ball is bounced from square four into square three to be caught by that player. The player in square three catches the ball and bounces it into square two for that player to catch, and so on around the grid. At any point a player with the ball can break the pattern and shout 'odds', 'evens' or 'primes'. They then can bounce the ball into an odd, even or prime numbered square of their choice.

If one of the four players makes a mistake then that player must leave their square. The other players advance to a higher numbered square and the player who made the mistake joins the game again in square 1.

Mistakes include:

- failing to bounce the ball into the correct square;
- allowing the ball to bounce more than once in their own square;
- hitting the ball out of bounds or onto a line;

- hitting the ball with a part of the body that does not include hands;
- hitting the ball out of turn.

The winner is the player in square 4 at the end of the game, which you can determine either with a time frame (egg timer) or the number of throws.

Visual representations: building blocks

There are a great variety of patterns which have been discovered over the centuries by mathematicians, as we have already learnt in this chapter. One of my favourites has to do with triangular numbers. The Greeks were interested in special numbers, such as triangular and square numbers, which can be represented visually using shapes, as seen in Figure 2.8.

Each subsequent number in the 'triangular number sequence' is created by adding a row to the bottom of the triangle. The next two triangular numbers are 21 (15 + 6) and 28 (21 + 7).

On 10 July 1796, when he was 19 years old, Carl Friedrich Gauss wrote in his diary: 'I have just proved this wonderful result that any natural number is the sum of three or fewer triangular numbers.'[6]

Throughout this chapter we have been looking at whole numbers. In mathematics we call these the 'natural numbers'. A natural number is defined to be any positive whole number, for example 1, 2, 3, 4, 5, 6, 7, etc.

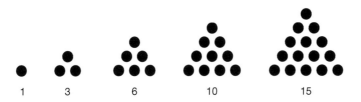

| 1 | 3 | 6 | 10 | 15 |

FIGURE 2.8 Triangular numbers

By looking at a few natural numbers you can see how they can be made up from triangular numbers. Below is a selection of natural numbers so you can start to see how Gauss's idea works.

$$2 = 1 + 1$$
$$5 = 3 + 1 + 1$$
$$12 = 10 + 1 + 1$$
$$19 = 10 + 6 + 3$$
$$25 = 21 + 3 + 1$$

With your class you can ask them to investigate Gauss's ideas further and find more natural numbers in the pattern to see how it progresses. In this way you are continually making connections between the concrete and the abstract and not falling into the trap of simply assuming your students are making these links.[7]

One other curiosity that involves triangular numbers, not to mention square and cube numbers, is the following pattern:

$$1 + 2 = 3$$
$$4 + 5 + 6 = 7 + 8$$
$$9 + 10 + 11 + 12 = 13 + 14 + 15$$
$$16 + 17 + 18 + 19 + 20 = 21 + 22 + 23 + 24$$

Notice that on both sides of the equal sign the addition of the numbers is the same, e.g. $4 + 5 + 6$ is 15 and so is $7 + 8$. This pattern continues to be true on all subsequent lines. In the above number curiosity you can ask your children what is special about the first numbers in every row and whether they can find any other number patterns.

MISCONCEPTIONS

Children can only think of numbers as symbols.

Some children believe that the single number name they say represents that number. This makes it important to use visual representations, such as with the triangular numbers seen in this chapter. Visual representations show the hidden beauty of numbers. Visualizations also help children to see number from a new perspective rather than only thinking of them as symbols. Children can also appreciate through multiple representations that there are many ways to explore number.

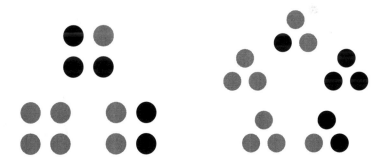

FIGURE 2.9 Visual illustrations of 12 as 3 × 4 and 15 as 5 × 3

NOTES

1 See Marland (1975), p. 100.
2 Depending on the ability of the class you could pick a smaller number between 20 and 99 to start and follow the same procedure above.
3 Gardner (1956) is the classic book on mathematical magic and has a whole section on the magic of digital roots.
4 Puzzles can be a good way to engage children in maths lessons. One of the great puzzle writers is Dudeney (1917). His puzzles are timeless and can still be used today.
5 See Humble (2013).
6 For an explanation of Gauss's proof see Humble (2002).
7 For research on why it is important to consider these links see Ball (1992).

Chapter 3

More and more Numbers

Don't count the days, make the days count.

Muhammad Ali

The last chapter hopefully started you to think about teaching number from a practical point of view. It provided a range of historical facts and how these could be related to lesson activities in a practical way. It has taken our journey from an exploration of the concrete outside world, as set out in Chapter 1, to looking at some of the abstract concepts in mathematics, all of course through our mathematical eyes.

As you have seen in the last chapter the range of maths activities you can do with just numbers is diverse.

And that was just the beginning.

We didn't have a chance to even consider fractions and decimals. But let's not repeat the Pythagoras remit that only whole numbers are meaningful and drown out anyone who disagrees. As I said, he lived in a different age. However, throughout my career I have met many students who would agree with Pythagoras – not to drown me – but who have a profound dislike and fear of fractions and decimals.

How can we avoid these anxieties and fears and make learning fractions and decimals more meaningful to students? Well, this chapter makes a start at doing this.

HISTORICAL BACKGROUND

Sometimes measurements need to be expressed with greater accuracy than whole numbers can allow. For example you may need to divide a whole number into a number of parts. This can be done through decimals and fractions.

However, it is often the case that fractions aren't given the importance they deserve. If we wish to divide something into a third then writing this as $\frac{1}{3}$ is more accurate than 0.33; the error in the calculation from fraction to decimal can easily be seen by using your calculator. Type in 1 ÷ 3 and then subtract 0.33 and you will find your calculator will show 0.00333. This shows that 0.33 is not the same as $\frac{1}{3}$.

The Egyptians did not use decimals at all and only used simple fractions. In Egyptian history the 'Eye of Horus' (see Figure 3.1) was used for the fractional measurement of the ingredients in medicines. Horus's eye was shattered into six pieces, each part thus representing the senses. The common fractional parts seen in the figure would have been useful for many calculations due to the fact that each fraction is a half of the previous one.

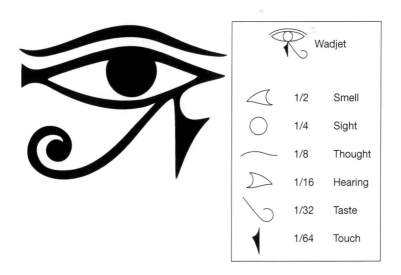

		Wadjet
	1/2	Smell
	1/4	Sight
	1/8	Thought
	1/16	Hearing
	1/32	Taste
	1/64	Touch

FIGURE 3.1 The Eye of Horus

The pieces in Horus's Eye add up to $\frac{63}{64}$ and some believe that the missing $\frac{1}{64}$ illustrates imperfection. These sorts of mystical properties are often found in numbers throughout history, such as in Leonardo Da Vinci's golden ratio or Chinese magic squares.

The Egyptians had notations for halves, thirds, quarters and sixths. When working with fractions in business, trade and banking the Egyptians expressed all their fractions as sums of unit fractions. A unit fraction always has a 1 on the top (the numerator, not the denominator, which is the number on the bottom). For example $\frac{3}{4}$ would be expressed as $\frac{1}{2} + \frac{1}{4}$ and $\frac{3}{8}$ as $\frac{1}{4} + \frac{1}{8}$. It is very important to stress that the denominator has to be different for all of the Egyptian unit fractions.

After discussing the Egyptian story with your class you can ask them to find groups of fractions that are equal to other fractions. You can challenge them by asking: how many different Egyptian fractions can you find in the same way that Egyptian merchants did 3,500–4,000 years ago?

Cuisenaire rods or fraction rods are useful resources that can be used to support activities such as these.

So how did the Greeks stand on fractions? Greek writers often expressed fractional values in words, for example Archimedes expressed the ratio of the circumference of a circle to its diameter as 'three diameters and part of one, the size of which lies between one seventh and ten seventy firsts'. We now would write this statement as $3\frac{1}{7} < \frac{C}{D} < 3\frac{10}{71}$. But writing fractions as words tended to create confusion as the reading of the fraction depended upon its context.

An Arabic author called Al-Hassar who lived in the twelfth century was the first to comment on the line used in fraction notation by instructing that 'the denominators be written below a horizontal line'. However, in Europe, it was not until the seventeenth century that the present day notation for fractions appeared.

CLASSROOM ACTIVITIES: FRACTIONS

Proportional parts

When teaching fractions a good place to start is to look at proportional parts, for example by dividing a shape into two halves in a variety of different ways. Ask your class to investigate the number of different ways this can be done. Figure 3.2 provides four examples that your class might come up with. You can challenge them to find as many different ways of dividing a shape into two equal parts and follow this activity with the hard task of looking for cases without lines of symmetry.

FIGURE 3.2 Dividing a shape into two

To extend this idea try the following:

- Divide a shape into four quarters in a variety of different ways.
- Divide a shape into thirds.
- Divide a shape into a number of unitary fractions so that it makes a whole.

Equivalent fractions

An important concept you'll need to teach your class concerning fractions is that of equivalent fractions. This means that the same fraction can be expressed in different forms. The example below shows a few of the many different ways of expressing one half as a fraction. I'm sure you can think of many more ways.

$$\frac{1}{2} = \frac{2}{4} = \frac{4}{8} = \frac{5}{10} = \frac{3}{6}$$

$\dfrac{1}{12}$	$\dfrac{2}{24}$	$\dfrac{4}{48}$	$\dfrac{5}{60}$
$\dfrac{1}{3}$	$\dfrac{3}{9}$	$\dfrac{4}{12}$	$\dfrac{5}{15}$
$\dfrac{1}{4}$	$\dfrac{3}{12}$	$\dfrac{6}{24}$	$\dfrac{12}{48}$
$\dfrac{1}{5}$	$\dfrac{2}{10}$	$\dfrac{5}{25}$	$\dfrac{7}{35}$

FIGURE 3.3 Equivalent fraction cards

This idea of equivalent fractions will be very important for children when they start to add fractions. A nice way of building these concepts is with a set of cards that show fractions and their equivalents. An example is shown in Figure 3.3.

To help children understand equivalent fractions try introducing this topic through a game of 'equivalent fraction snap'. You will need to make four cards featuring the same fraction but in different forms. It would be good to have at least 40 cards and hence ten fractions. Players deal two cards and call 'snap' if they are equivalent. If not they are put back on the bottom of their pile of cards. The player who wins the most snaps is the winner.

Many resource catalogues sell fraction cards, however children learn much more by making their own; by doing this children will have a greater understanding of what 'equivalence' means. Why not make your own fraction snap game?

Adding fractions

Now that your children are confident with equivalent fractions and proportional parts they are ready to try adding and subtracting fractions. One way to develop their understanding is to teach this in a visual way. It is good to have different strategies that you can use to solve a problem, and by giving your students a 'tool box' of strategies you offer them a greater range of opportunities to learn. Also you will find that some children will store a visual method in their memory better than a written one and vice versa.

Here is how you add fractions using pictures. Think about the fractions in a visual way as proportional parts of a whole. A half means you are dividing the shape into two parts, and so looks like Figure 3.4.

■ **FIGURE 3.4** Visual representation of a half

One-third means you are dividing the shape into three parts, which would look like Figure 3.5.

■ **FIGURE 3.5** Visual representation of a third

Notice that in Figure 14 the shape has been divided vertically and in Figure 3.5 horizontally. You need to do this because adding these two fractions together is the same as overlapping the two grids.

and   gives

FIGURE 3.6 Overlapping grid for addition of fractions

Notice that in Figure 3.6 the vertical grid overlaps the horizontal grid, creating the sections that give you the common denominator needed for adding two fractions.

The final grid shows you that one half is proportional to three squares in this sum and one-third is two squares. Using these proportions in the final grid you can find the answer to the addition of $\frac{1}{2} + \frac{1}{3}$.

We need to shade in three squares for the $\frac{1}{2}$ and two squares for the $\frac{1}{3}$. You can't shade in a square more than once. You can see from the answer grid in Figure 3.7 that five squares are shaded out of six, so the answer is $\frac{5}{6}$.

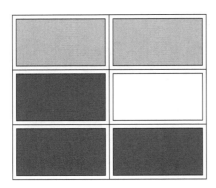

FIGURE 3.7 Addition using visual methods

The traditional written method for fraction addition would lead you to write the fractions in their equivalent forms using a common denominator:

$$\frac{1}{2} + \frac{1}{3} = \frac{3}{6} + \frac{2}{6}$$

then to add these fractions:

$$\frac{3}{6} + \frac{2}{6} = \frac{5}{6}$$

The same method can be used with any fraction addition sum. For example $\frac{1}{3} + \frac{2}{5}$ would be represented as in Figure 3.8. The final grid is made up of a 'common denominator' of 15 squares. This gives an answer of $\frac{11}{15}$, as shown in Figure 3.8, by totalling the shaded squares when you perform the addition sum.

Now try to work out the equivalent fractions for $\frac{1}{3}$ and $\frac{2}{5}$, and use the traditional written method to add these fractions. You should get the same answer.

FIGURE 3.8 Visual method to calculate $\frac{1}{3} + \frac{2}{5}$

The visual method described above is not designed to replace the traditional written method but merely to support learners on their journey to understand the addition and subtraction of fractions.

This is a good point now to put down the book, pick up a pencil and paper and create your addition and subtraction questions. You should do these questions using both of the methods described above in order to confirm that both methods give you the same answer.

CLASSROOM ACTIVITIES: DECIMALS

Maybe you did not know, but there are different sorts of decimals. There are decimals that can be written as fractions. These are called rational numbers. Examples of rational numbers are 0.5 = $\frac{1}{2}$ and 0.25 = $\frac{1}{4}$.

There are 'beautiful' decimals that repeat after a number of digits. These are called cyclic decimals. The decimal equivalent of $\frac{1}{7}$ is a cyclic decimal. It has a number that repeats after six decimal places.

$$\frac{1}{7} = 0.14285714285714285714\ldots$$

$$\frac{2}{7} = 0.285714285714285714\ldots$$

Notice that these sevenths have similar repeating patterns. Try other sevenths on your calculator and you will see the same numbers appearing in the decimal but at a different cyclic position.

Here is another example of a cyclic decimal, and this one repeats after 16 decimal places.

$$\frac{1}{17} = 0.0588235941176470588\ldots$$

In fact if the number on the bottom of the fraction (denominator) is a prime number then there will be recurring digits.

There are also other decimals that cannot be written as fractions. These are called irrationals. The majority of irrational numbers are square roots.

We can draw a Venn diagram to show how all these different numbers fit together (Figure 3.9).

You can use Venn diagrams with children as a way of sorting and classifying, not only numbers, but a range of different objects, as shown in Figure 20.

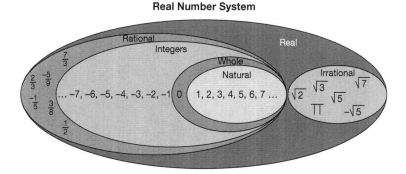

FIGURE 3.9 Venn diagram showing the set of all real numbers

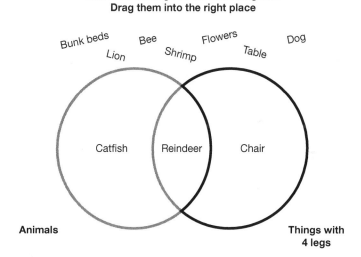

FIGURE 3.10 Examples of a Venn diagram

Calculators and decimals

Calculators can seem very mysterious to children. They often make mistakes by pressing the wrong buttons and, because they have no concept of the size of the answer, they do not realize the result the calculator gives is wrong. One way to try to overcome this initial difficulty is for you to tell your class that they should try to think of an approximate answer for their calculation. For example, if the question was 237 × 619, the children should think about the answer being approximately 200 × 600, which is 120,000. They can then use this approximation to compare the answer on their calculator to ensure they have pressed the right buttons in the first place. Another good check is for children simply to do the calculation twice with the numbers reversed, i.e. 619 × 237. Not only does this check the answer but it also shows the multiplication has a commutative property.

Test your calculator

Let's put your calculator through its paces. Why? First, it is fun for your children to do and allows them to explore cyclic fractions on their calculators. This idea of experimenting with cyclic fractions on their calculators will help them to understand repeating patterns. Second, it reinforces the concept of multiplying a decimal by ten. Third, it shows how powerful the calculator's processor is.

A test you can perform in order to check the quality of any calculator is to enter the sum: 1 divided by 7. The number of digits your calculator stores hidden off the screen gives a measure of the quality of the calculator. While doing the following test you should write down the display shown on the calculator after each calculation. Right, so back to the test.

First 1 divided by 7 will give you the cyclic decimal
0.1428571428 . . .

↓

Multiply this answer (0.1428571428 . . .) by 10 and subtract the first digit, in this case 1, to get 0.4285714285 . . .

↓

Multiply this answer by 10 and subtract the 4 to get
0.2857142857 . . .

↓

Multiply this answer by 10 and subtract the 2, and so on, until no more new hidden digits appear.

How many answers did you write down? The more times you had to do this, the better your calculator's processor. How did your calculator fare in this test? You will find that the processor in some mobile phone calculators is much better than your standard classroom calculator.

This does not mean that some calculators will not give you the right answer. All it means is that if you were doing very large or very small calculations then you may get errors in the last few digits of the calculation. But for most day-to-day uses we don't have to perform calculations that involve more than ten digits.

Division with decimal answers

Young children often find division difficult. What can we do about this? Let's look at an example you can do with your class and think about the best way to approach it. You might want your children to do this question first without you scaffolding any support. This will highlight for you any problems your class may have and allow you to look for misconceptions that can be addressed.

Divide 23 sweets among 4 children

When you divide 23 sweets among 4 children, you would start by sharing out 5 sweets to each of the 4 children and then keep 3 left over as possible special treats for the future. In doing this you have divided 23 by 4 and obtained an answer of 5 remainder 3.

Now let's do the same calculation but using different units.

Divide 23 kilograms of coal among 4 households

47

When you divide 23 kg among 4 households you start by giving 5 kg to each household. But instead of writing a remainder of 3 you would have written a fraction – three-quarters of a kilogram – or a decimal – 0.75 kg or 750 g.

Sometimes this is where the problem arises. It's not that children do not know how to divide, it's all the other stuff that comes with a division calculation: remainders, fractions, decimals and units of measurement. My advice would be to take it one step at a time. If you can find out how many whole parts go into the number you're virtually home and dry.

An easy method to do this is called 'chunking'. This method works by sharing out the number you want to divide into parts. Say we are asked to calculate 165 divided by 6.

$$165 \div 6$$

You start by working out the 6 times table, and find how many multiples of 6 go into 165. We know $10 \times 6 = 60$ and so $2 \times 60 = 20 \times 6 = 120$, you can see that we are getting closer to the answer. $30 \times 6 = 180$ is too much. How much more do we need to get to 165? Well, it's $165 - 120$, which is 45. Now do the process again with the 6 times table for 45. We know $2 \times 6 = 12$, $4 \times 6 = 24$, $6 \times 6 = 36$, $7 \times 6 = 42$.

We now have

$$20 \times 6 = 120$$
$$7 \times 6 = 42$$

Adding these gives

$$27 \times 6 = 162$$

The answer to the question $165 \div 6$ is that 6 goes 27 times into 162, therefore to get to 165 we have a remainder of 3.

With the chunking method you break up the question into chunks. Whatever the remainder is you can turn it into a decimal by dividing it by the divisor. In this case we would divide 3 by 6 to get 0.5.

Alongside chunking there are a range of other methods, including traditional division methods for performing calculations, as the one above. A number of children who find division difficult can benefit from foundation work in methods such as chunking. These methods are not designed to be used by the child throughout their mathematical development: they are merely supportive stopping points along a journey that enables them to improve their confidence and competency with division techniques.

I will finish this section by looking at a method that is very similar to chunking, which I have seen a number of children use successfully, and which is called 'repeated subtraction'. It tackles the problem in a slightly different way but using a similar approach.

To illustrate, we will now do the same division we did using chunking but now using repeated subtraction. This method involves subtracting multiples of the divisor from the numerator.

$165 \div 6$

The most basic strategy a child could have would be to take repeatedly 6 away from 165. He or she would have to do this 27 times. Improvements in the child's strategy would allow him or her to think of initially taking multiples of 60 (because that is 10×6) away from 165 (see Figure 3.11 on how to notate this). The child would know that 2 lots of 60 would leave 45. They could then use another 'optimum' strategy of taking away maybe 30 (because that is 5×6) to get closer to the answer. The 10s and the 5 are placed alongside the subtraction to show the child how many times 6 has been subtracted.

```
165
 -60        10
―――
105
 -60        10
―――
 45
 -30         5
―――
 15
 -12         2
―――
  r3    Total 27
```

FIGURE 3.11 Repeated subtraction

Applications of decimals: carbon footprint

Real life calculations with decimals can motivate children. Looking at topical issues such as 'carbon footprint' can give opportunities for children to use decimals. Let's look at an example. A typical carbon footprint calculator is shown in Table 3.1, giving the averages for household carbon dioxide (CO_2).

TABLE 3.1 Carbon footprint calculator

	UK average household CO_2 (tonnes)
Gas, oil and coal	1.62
Electricity	1.30
Private car	1.08
Public transport	0.36
Holiday flights	0.65
Food and drink	0.59
Clothes and shoes	0.49
Car manufacture	0.72
Buildings, furniture and appliances	0.98
Recreation and services	1.55
Finance and other services	0.36
Share of public services	1.28
Total footprint	10.96

Source: www.carbonfootprint.com

A carbon footprint is a measure of the amount of CO_2 emitted through the combustion of fossil fuels on a yearly basis. CO_2 is recognized as a greenhouse gas, of which increasing levels in the atmosphere are linked to global warming and climate change. It is also increasingly used as a measure of our impact on the environment.

The activities that affect the carbon footprint of individuals vary according to a number of factors. For example, car travel depends on distance driven, fuel efficiency and number of passengers per vehicle. Electricity use depends on the size of the household and usage patterns. Food and drink depends on whether you are a meat-eater, vegetarian or vegan, use conventionally farmed foods or organic produce.

All of these have carbon conversion factors to indicate the amount of CO_2 produced by the activity in kilograms. For example, a car produces 0.21 kg of CO_2 per person per kilometre, whereas a bus produces 0.09 kg of CO_2 per person per kilometre travelled. Using this sort of information the carbon footprint calculator can calculate your total CO_2 emissions for travel. Similar methods are used for other contributing factors.

Walkers Crisps was the first company to put carbon footprint figures on their products. These figures were calculated by the Carbon Trust, a private company set up by the government to reduce the UK's carbon footprint. The Trust spent several

TABLE 3.2 Carbon emissions by transport

Transport	Carbon emissions (kg of CO_2 per person per km)
Walk	0.00
Bicycle	0.00
Bus	0.09
Train	0.06
Motorbike	0.10
Car	0.21
Plane	0.16

months working out that 75 g of greenhouse gases are given off in the production of a 33.5 g bag of Walkers crisps. It took into account the energy used in the farming, manufacture, packaging, distribution and finally the disposal of the packet.

By giving your class information such as the above you can set up a real life investigation project that will involve performing a whole range of decimal calculations. This will bring all of the students' decimal skills to life and make them meaningful. When you revisit the topic of decimals in the future with the class you can ask them if they remember the carbon footprint project. This will trigger transfer memories from the past from which you can draw.

MISCONCEPTIONS

Division

The interpretation of a division as a remainder, fraction and decimal will cause many children issues. For example:

$9 \div 4$ is equal to 2 remainder 1, which can be written as $2\frac{1}{4}$ or 2.25.

However, a common mistake made by children is to say $9 \div 4$ is 2.1, which is putting the remainder as the decimal rather than converting the remainder into either a decimal or a fractional part.

Chapter 4

On the journey

Measurement

We do not follow maps to buried treasure and X never, ever marks the spot.

Indiana Jones to his students in the *Last Crusade*

The last two chapters focused on number and classroom activities to help you teach using a practical approach. In Chapter 2 we looked at whole numbers and progressed along our journey in Chapter 3 to divide these into their fractional parts. With measurement it is natural to think about the units involved in measuring in the same way as we have with numbers. A child needs to understand how to divide a unit of measurement into its parts, e.g. time into minutes, hours or seconds; or lengths into metres, centimetres or millimetres. This chapter begins by looking at how the standardization of measurement has evolved over time. This is followed by more ideas regarding how to devise inventive classroom sessions on measurement.

HISTORICAL BACKGROUND

Time and travel were often linked in the past. Distances were expressed as 'moons away' or 'from sunrise to sunset'. We can bring time to life by looking at the historical background to why we have watches and even why we want to order the day into the pattern of hours, minutes and seconds.

The first measurement of time was based on natural events that occur at regular intervals. The Babylonians created a 'calendar' of 360 days by considering the patterns of night and day and the seasons. They counted in multiples of 12 and 60. They used 60 as their starting point when counting, just as we use 10 in our counting system. Babylonian numbers are shown in Figure 2.1 on page 18.

The Babylonians divided their day into 24 hours, each hour having 60 minutes, and each minute having 60 seconds. This measure of counting time has survived for over 4,000 years and we still use it today.

Regarding time measurement, it wasn't until 1855 in Britain that Greenwich Mean Time (GMT) was set on the majority of clocks throughout the land. This was a necessity to allow the efficient running of the ever important and growing railway network in the UK.

Hours turn into days, days turn into weeks, weeks turn into months. That's why we have calendars. The Babylonians designed the first calendar, but the Egyptians believed that their system needed to be adapted and added five feast days to each year. In 46 BC the Romans initiated the leap year and added a day every four years in February to make their Julian calendar more accurate. It was not until 1752 that the Gregorian calendar, created by Pope Gregory XIII, replaced this Roman calendar in Britain, and we still use it today.

In ancient times the body was used to set measurements of length. Today we call these non-standard units. The body parts included the length of an average man's foot (the foot), the width of a man's thumb (the inch), the width of a hand (the hand), the length of a hand outstretched (the span), the length of a man's belt (the yard) and the length of a double step (the pace). Understandably these units caused a great deal of problems when it came to standardization. One man's foot can be very different from another's! This standardization came about in 1795 with the creation of the French metric measurement system, which included the litre, the gram and the metre.

CLASSROOM ACTIVITIES: LENGTH AND DISTANCE

In everyday life we all make use of measurement in our homes, local environment, playing sports and games, and in finding our way from A to B. The measurements are today all in standard units. Standard units have been created to allow consistency and the ability for people to communicate measures.

The names of units become more meaningful to children as they develop their own memories linked to these units. For example, being measured as they grow in metres and centimetres or their weight fluctuating in kilograms and grams. A child's understanding and development with measuring needs to include the tools required to measure different quantities such as:

How far is it from school to your home?
How tall is your teacher?
How far is the nearest seaside?
How thick is a sheet of paper?
How wide is your classroom?

These are the sorts of questions you can ask your class to start them thinking about length and distance. Then ask the class what instruments would be needed for them to be able to answer the questions:

How wide is your classroom?
What do we need to measure this with?
Would you use a 30 cm ruler, a metre rule, a 3 m tape measure, or a trundle wheel?
Which is the most appropriate to give the best level of accuracy?

When the children are giving their answers it is always good to find out from them how accurate they feel using different instruments will be. Will the answer given by the instrument be correct to the nearest metre, nearest centimetre, millimetre or tenth of a millimetre? Decisions such as these offer teaching opportunities and chances for the class to think about what accuracy of measurement means.

Let's look at some possible triggers that can help students remember and see connections regarding measurement.

The Abominable Snowman: length

The Abominable Snowman, or the Yeti, is believed to live in Nepal. No one has yet proved its existence and it remains a creature of myth and folklore. Occasionally people say they have seen a large animal or seen odd footprints. In 2007 an American television crew claimed to have found the Yeti's tracks not far from Mount Everest. Josh Gates, host of a Sci-Fi channel series, claimed that he found three mysterious footprints. One of these footprints measured about 13 inches long and was about the same width at the widest point.

Taking this story you could ask your students: what might the Abominable Snowman look like and how tall would he be?

By measuring the relative size of your foot to your height, you can use this ratio to help you estimate the height of the Abominable Snowman.

Students can then draw graphs to illustrate the foot sizes and heights of everyone in their class. Look at the width of children's feet in the class and see if this is connected to their height. The children can use the data they have collected to help estimate the height of the Abominable Snowman.

Maybe you want to do the same lesson but with fantasy monsters or dinosaurs. You can give your class pieces of information to allow them to investigate these ideas further. An example using a dinosaur could be as follows: 'a tyrannosaurus dinosaur's footprint found in Mexico on 18 December 2007 measured 83 cm long by 71 cm wide. These dinosaurs were thought to weigh up to 6.5 tonnes and stand 4 m tall.'

FIGURE 4.1 Dinosaur footprint

Accompanying this information give the class some life-size footprints of other dinosaurs and ask them to work out how long, wide, tall and heavy that dinosaur might have been, taking the tyrannosaurus as an example.

We have just carried out a lesson on length, height, weight and ratio from an engaging point of view of monster footprints. This is a much more stimulating and memorable way to teach measurement. The class is much more likely to remember the work they have done using dinosaurs as a way of learning about different measurement units.

Peter Rabbit: distance

An inventive activity to help develop your class's positional language is to create your own maths journey.[1] This relates back to Chapter 1 and how we view the world. Using a map of your local area you can illustrate how to give directions to travel from one point to another. You can discuss with the class if they have seen their Mum or Dad giving directions to someone to find a place and the type of words they used to do this, leading nicely to directions and distance measurement.

You can use a storybook to stimulate and set the scene. In the example below the story of Peter Rabbit is used to act as a springboard for a lesson on direction and distance.

In the story, Peter Rabbit is lost in a garden maze. Determine which way he must move around in the garden to get home without crossing the path of Mr McGregor.

Devise a map of Mr McGregor's garden. Give this to your class. Write down instructions for Peter Rabbit's journey home, including measurements and directions for avoiding Mr McGregor along the way. These measurements can be non-standard, such as footsteps. The map does not need to be drawn on a piece of paper: you can use the tables and chairs in your classroom to set out the cabbage patch, the carrot plot and the rest of Mr McGregor's garden.

When the children have completed this task you can ask them to write down Peter Rabbit's route as a series of instructions.

FIGURE 4.2 Carrots from Mr McGregor's garden

The whole act of giving them the responsibility of mapping out the route is providing them with the opportunity for ownership, which, as you are beginning to realize from the chapters that have gone before, is very important.

The good thing about certain activities is that they are not age dependent. You just choose a relevant story that will stimulate children's imaginations. With older children you can do the same activity with robots or even the dreaded zombies.

CLASSROOM ACTIVITIES: TIME

We are now moving onto another very important measurement that children need to feel happy with in many ways; not only from a mathematics standpoint but also for everyday life activities.

▓ **FIGURE 4.3** Clocks

Time regulates our lives, providing us with a pattern for our days: a time to get up, a time to be at school, a time to eat, a time to start the lesson, a time to catch the bus. We are logical mathematical creatures living in an ordered world.

It is important to be able to sequence events in chronological order so that children understand the patterns of time.

There are three uses of time that you need to teach your class. These are:

- historical time:
- time taken;
- time telling.

Historical time concerns chronology and therefore the use of time lines to illustrate this. You can start to think about chronological events by talking about birthdays and holidays.

Time taken is about measuring the duration of an event; examples include journeys, lesson length and doing something in a set time. Using clocks, watches and calendars come under the topic of telling time.

Cartoon time: historical time

We can help children appreciate the patterns that exist in the world by looking at the way their own life has a pattern. They can do this by examining how their own day is ordered. Ask your class to create a set of cartoon images to show the sequence of events in their day. They then cut these out and jumble them up. The activity you set is for them to put the images back in the correct chronological order.

Similarly you can take an everyday activity, such as having breakfast, and ask the class to give a possible correct order to it, e.g. making breakfast: get out bowl, pick cereal, pour into bowl, add milk, get spoon, take to table, eat, take to sink, wash, dry, put back in cupboard, etc.

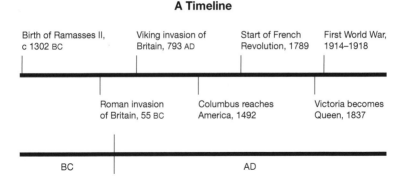

FIGURE 4.4 Historical timeline

Measuring devices: time taken

Use a range of different measuring devices in inventive ways. First, try measuring the time taken for a single event. You could use egg timers, sand clocks, water clocks, candle clocks, metronomes or pendulums. Questions could include:

- How many clicks of a metronome does it take for you to walk around the classroom?
- How far does the candle burn down while you read a nursery rhyme?
- How many turns of the egg timer does it take for your friend to walk around the playground?
- How many skips can you do in 30 drips of a water clock?
- How many bounces of a ball can you do in one turn of the sand clock?

Second, make a comparison of the difference in time taken to carry out two separate events. You can also ask your class to think of separate activities they can time and then make comparisons, such as ten skips and ten bounces of a ball; or putting on a pair of wellies and putting on a pair of shoes.

They then need to time each of the events using one of the measuring devices above so as to compare the amount of time each takes.

Sundial and Chinese New Year: time telling

Sundial

There are many different types of sundials. They all work using mathematical principles. There is a good introductory chapter in *Mathematics Galore*[2] on sundials, which looks at the mathematics behind the workings of these devices. There are different types of human sundials. One such is the 'analemmatic sundial' (Figure 4.5) where the user stands at a central marked position and his or her shadow points to the correct marked hour of the day.

▧ **FIGURE 4.5** Analemmatic sundial

With your class you can use the concept of human sundials. The length of a human shadow can be used to measure the Sun's elevation and show the time at any point in the day. In order to investigate this, take your class outside at different times of the day. Ask the children to take it in turns to measures the length of their partner's shadow. Record these measurements on a graph. Each child will have his or her own graph of shadow length against time of day recorded. You can tell the children that this is the way our ancestors used to calculate the passing of time before the invention of clocks.

Other primitive forms of time keeping are water and sand clocks. A challenge you can give to your students is to create a clock that would measure the passing of 30 seconds, asking how much sand or water would be required.

Chinese New Year

Looking at other countries, customs and cultures can make learning time-telling more meaningful to children. Why not use something very colourful such as the Chinese New Year and zodiac to inspire your class's imagination with time?

The Chinese celebrate New Year on 23 January each year, marking the end of the winter season and the beginning of spring. Each year has an animal associated with it. The zodiac animals originate from star patterns seen in the night sky. The Chinese believe that these 12 zodiac animals can offer insights into the personality of those people born that year. The 12 animal years rotate in a cyclic pattern, with 2013 being the year of the Snake (the beginning of the cyclical pattern).

Here are the twelve Chinese zodiac animal signs:

1. Snake – charming and captivating
2. Horse – ambitious and full of strength
3. Ram – hard working and patient
4. Monkey – intelligent and quick

5. Rooster – courageous and creative
6. Dog – honest and friendly
7. Pig – generous and peaceful
8. Rat – intelligent and energetic
9. Ox – hard working and patient
10. Tiger – enthusiastic and determined
11. Rabbit – friendly and generous
12. Dragon – enthusiastic and self-confident

As you have seen in Chapter 3 when looking at cyclic decimals such as $\frac{1}{7}$ (which repeats every six digits), the pattern of the Chinese zodiac also repeats in a cyclic order, but repeating its pattern every 12 years.

FIGURE 4.6 Chinese zodiac

FIGURE 4.7 Lunar phases

Using the Chinese zodiac in a lesson, start by asking the children to discover which is their own birth sign. From this they can then try to calculate their brother's and sister's animal signs. Ask the class to think of other patterns that repeat in a cycle. Hopefully they will think of sunrise, sunset, days of the week, months in the year, the moon's shape (lunar phases).

To embed the learning of repeating patterns the children can create drawings or symbols to represent a cyclical pattern. This could be a pattern they see around them or a pattern they design using blocks. As we will see in Chapter 7 on algebra, this is the start of a journey to abstraction.

MISCONCEPTIONS

Many children have difficulty accepting that all measurement is approximate because ever-smaller units can be used to gain greater accuracy. Experience with approximation and accuracy through activities will help them to accept and feel more comfortable about estimates and level of exactness. Estimates should never be regarded as 'wrong' merely because they can be improved with more detailed measurement.

NOTES

1 My 'Dr Maths explorer puzzle' books use the mathematical language of journeys to help teach basic number work (Humble 2012–2014).
2 Budd and Sangwin (2001)

Chapter 5

Many paths to take
Geometry

> The real voyage of discovery consists not in seeking new land-
> scapes, but in having new eyes.
>
> *In Search of Lost Time* by Marcel Proust

In the last chapter I considered units that have been developed to improve accuracy and uniformity so as to standardize meas-urement. This continued our journey from Chapter 3, which looked at fractional parts of a whole. We now need to take measurement into two and three dimensions and focus on the shapes that children are required to learn in their maths lessons. Geometry is a visual topic and therefore in this chapter I will reflect back to some of the concepts set out in Chapter 1. You will need to open your mathematical eyes for this chapter as geometry is all about objects, shapes, their properties and relations. Let's begin with a look at Plato, Euclid and Kepler's geometric discoveries and then take a walk into the world of geometry.

HISTORICAL BACKGROUND

The word 'geometry' comes from the Greek word meaning 'earth measurement'. In ancient Greece people were required to survey the land and they did this by laying out shapes, each of which could be measured.

As discussed in Chapter 1 the Greek mathematician Euclid gathered together the properties of geometrical shapes in his epic book called *Euclid's Elements*. Euclid was a unifier of information on geometry at that time, gathering together in one place all the information that was then known. There have been other mathematical figures, such as Sir Isaac Newton, Carl Friedrich Gauss, James Clerk Maxwell, Leonhard Euler and Albert Einstein, who were also unifiers. At their respective times in history they brought together the information that was known and allowed mathematical theory to develop further.

Plato, around 400 BC, gave the five regular polyhedra a mystical significance, because each of these three-dimensional (3D) shapes is made using a single two-dimensional (2D) shape. Plato's five 3D shapes are called the Platonic solids, in honour of his discovery. Plato discovered that there are only five 3D objects that can be made from one 2D figure that forms all of its faces. These are the:

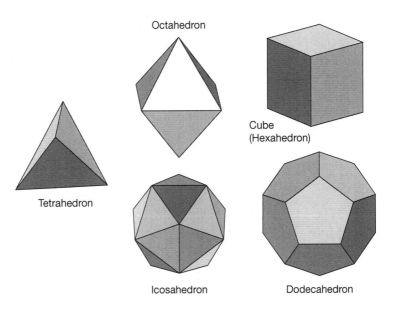

FIGURE 5.1 Platonic solids

- Tetrahedron – made up of triangles;
- Octahedron – made up of triangles;
- Cube – made up of squares;
- Icosahedron – made up of triangles;
- Dodecahedron – made up of pentagons.

In the 1600s the German Johannes Kepler created his theory of how the planets move around the Sun by using Plato's facts about the Platonic solids in his calculations. He thought that the Platonic solids fitted inside each other, rather like Russian nesting dolls. Unfortunately his idea wasn't quite right. It has since been shown that the planets move on elliptical paths. However, you can understand why Kepler would have believed this to be true, as his nesting Platonic solids would have created a very pretty solar system as viewed by mathematical eyes.

We live in a 3D world. All shapes are 3D as they have length, width and depth. It is important for children to be able to recognize and name shapes, as our world is full of them.

CLASSROOM ACTIVITIES: GEOMETRY

Shape art

There are a number of artists who use standard 2D shapes to create their pictures and paintings. Think about creating a display in your classroom of mathematical art that uses this technique. You could even make an exhibition programme featuring your chosen artists and paintings. In the programme you could include historical data alongside mathematical facts about the construction of the painting, where it is displayed and its present value. Once inspired ask your students to create their own mathematical paintings to display in their very own exhibition for other classes in the school to come and see.[1]

The art they create could involve certain shapes, as shown in the painting by Paul Klee shown in Figure 5.2. As part of the art/maths project they will investigate and find out as much as

FIGURE 5.2 'Quarry' by Paul Klee
Source: Zentrum Paul Klee Bern Museum collection, www.emuseum.zpk.org

they can about the properties of these shapes (equal sides, angles, symmetry lines, rotational symmetries, etc.).

Josef Albers's paintings often involve squares of various sizes. One such famous painting, called *Homage to the Square*, when last sold in 2007 at Sotheby's, made $1.5 million.

Alternatively the artist Andy Goldsworthy uses natural materials to create his art, such as stones, mud, flowers, leaves and twigs.

Goldsworthy's art, in Figure 5.3, shows an egg shape made of bricks (an egg shape is called a Cassini oval) and a circle made from straight twigs and branches (shown in a curved stitching pattern). The outdoor environment is a rich place for learning and contains many mathematical resources readily available to explore. Andy Goldsworthy's work offers some great

Early morning calm
knotweed stalks
pushed into lake bottom
made complete by their own reflections
Derwent Water, Cumbria, 20 February and 8–9 March, 1988

Culvert Cairn
Private Collection, California, US, 2013

FIGURE 5.3 Andy Goldsworthy's art

starting points for maths education outside the classroom. Using a collection of different sized pebbles create your own maths sculpture. When the children have all had an opportunity to create a piece of art, ask what is the same and what is different about the various sculptures. You can include the natural world's fractal maths from Chapter 1.

Shapes around you

Moving on from looking at shapes used in art you can encourage children to find shapes they see in the world around them and then discuss the differences and similarities between them. This revisits ideas we looked at in Chapter 1 regarding using your mathematical eyes on a maths walk.

To start, let's play a game in class and ask the children: how many shapes can you see? This is a bit like 'I Spy shape'. This will help reinforce shape recognition. The children should be able to name and locate as many shapes as possible, not just ones that have been located on the wall, but within objects, such as the desks, the windows, the door, the floor.

A useful way to collect and organize the data is by using a tick list or tally chart. The children need to be aware of the properties of these shapes, including the number of sides, type of symmetry and whether the shape is regular or irregular.

Now that the children have identified shapes in their I Spy game they can play in partners a game to compare pairs of shapes. They can take turns describing properties the two shapes share and then look for ways in which they differ, until no further properties can be found.

Shopping shapes

We buy products in boxes and cartons. Once we have eaten the food or emptied the contents we typically throw the packaging away. Studying the geometry of various container shapes offers an opportunity to investigate the mathematics of packaging. Food cartons and packages are 3D in shape. Your class can collect different boxes and cartons to bring to school, once washed out!

When working with younger children start by giving them a collection of 3D shapes that you would find in a typical shopping bag. Get them to sort the packages in a variety of ways so that they become aware of different properties. Sorting could include by colour, shape, size, and if it can roll and be used to build a structure.

With older children start by creating an area in the classroom that becomes your supermarket table. Over a period of time they try to collect as many different 3D shapes they can spot while shopping.

Once the table is as complete as you want, start asking questions such as these:

- Which box holds the most?
- Which box holds the least?
- Which box has the greatest amount of red colouring on its surface? Expressed as a percentage?
- Which shaped boxes fit together best?
- Why do certain groups of boxes fit together? What are their internal angles?
- If you had to pack an international aid box how many shapes could you fit with the minimum space left over?
- When products are being delivered to your supermarket what are the problems the haulier might experience with certain packages?

Once the investigation around packaging is coming to an end you could start to discuss how the manufacturers put the shapes together. This brings into your lesson area, volume and nets. Taking apart a cube (that might have been used for containing chocolates), the children can see how the mathematical net is put together (Figure 5.4).

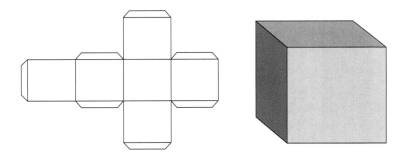

■ FIGURE 5.4 Net of a cube

For homework the children can carry out a home survey looking at their own household's weekly shop. They would need to record the products bought and the types of packaging used. This project could link to environmentally friendly usage and the disposal of packaging. Your class can introduce ways of reducing packaging sizes and minimizing waste.

Tessellations

A tessellation is defined as tiling a flat surface using one or more geometric shapes, with no overlaps or gaps. Maurits Escher[2] was a Dutch graphic artist of the twentieth century who created a number of beautiful mathematically inspired paintings.

To start, show your class some examples of Escher's tessellation art. Then ask them to investigate why some shapes tessellate and others don't. You can see from Figure 5.6 that tessellation will occur with regular 2D shapes whose internal angles are a factor of 360 degrees.

There are tessellations that can be made up of more than one shape, as seen in the examples of tessellations in Figure 5.5.

Hexiamonds are created by joining six identical equilateral triangles side by side. There are exactly 12 different possible ways you can do this as shown in Figure 5.7.

FIGURE 5.5 Tessellations and art: examples of different kinds of tessellations

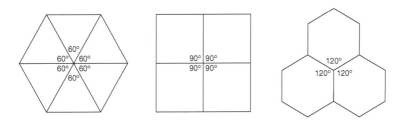

FIGURE 5.6 Regular two-dimensional tessellated polygons

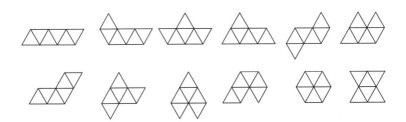

FIGURE 5.7 The 12 possible hexiamonds

It is fun to challenge children to make various pictures using these shapes so challenge your class to do this. Once the children have had the opportunity to create some of these pictures, they can then design some of their own shapes using hexiamonds or other shape tessellations. The children can then colour, cut out and use different shapes to create a collage tessellating picture (see Figure 5.8 for examples). But remember, it is important to ask them to 'do the maths' part of this art work and write all they know about the properties of the shapes they have used in their maths art.

Alphabet symmetry

It is always important to relate children's school mathematics to experiences in their own world. Using the alphabet is one way to start a symmetry lesson. This helps children realize they are not learning maths in isolation to other subjects.

Letters A and C have mirror symmetry in the vertical and horizontal directions respectively. The letter Z has rotational symmetry order 2, as it looks the same after it has been rotated by 180 degrees. The letter X by contrast has both rotational and mirror symmetries (Figure 5.9).

In order for your class to investigate vertical, horizontal and rotational symmetry ask the children to write down their own name in capital letters. They can start to do this by writing the letters as they are shown reflected in a mirror.

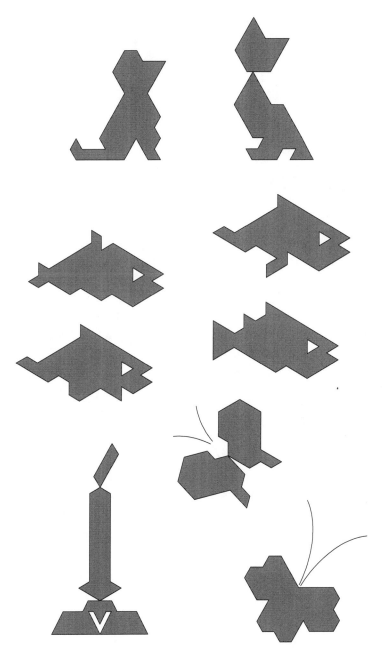

FIGURE 5.8 Hexiamond pictures

A B C D E
F G H I J K
L M N O P
Q R S T U
V W X Y Z

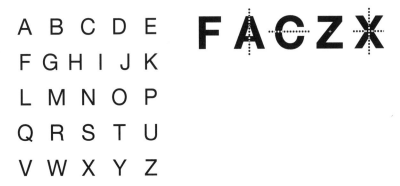

FIGURE 5.9 Alphabet symmetry

If you want to take this lesson further you could get them to create a 'secret symmetry code alphabet' which they could use to pretend they are being 'symmetry spies'.

Here is a possible way to make a 'mirror code'. The letters with vertical line symmetry lose the right half of their shape, and letters that do not have vertical symmetry are turned upside down. See Table 5.1 for how this code works for the first few letters of the alphabet.

TABLE 5.1 Mirror code

A	B	C	D	E	F	G	H	I
⊦	ᗺ	Ɔ	ᗡ	Ǝ	⅁Ⅎ	⅁	⊦	I

Here is an extra challenge question you can set regarding the 26 letters of the alphabet.

Find the letters in this alphabet challenge:

- Seven letters that have vertical mirror symmetry.
- Five letters that have horizontal mirror symmetry.

- Four letters that have both horizontal and vertical mirror symmetry.
- Three letters that only have rotational symmetry.
- Seven letters that have no symmetry (asymmetric letters).

MISCONCEPTIONS

Children often have an image of what a triangle looks like. They typically imagine it as an equilateral triangle. As a consequence an error that may result is not being able to recognize other triangular shapes because they are not in a typical orientation. Similarly, with other shapes, children will always have an image of a regular type, not an irregular version. For example when told to find a pentagon they might believe all pentagons are regular five-sided figures. This is not the case, as shown in Figure 5.10.

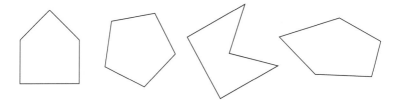

FIGURE 5.10 Pentagons

NOTES

1 Gattegno (1971) discusses student ownership of their learning and the act of 'doing' contrasted with teaching that is 'done to' children.
2 Hofstadter (1979) relates Escher's work to mathematical creativity.

Chapter 6

Ownership
Statistics and probability

> When you have eliminated the impossible, whatever remains, however improbable must be the truth.
>
> Sherlock Holmes in *The Signal Four*
> by Sir Arthur Conan Doyle

Now you have reached this point in the journey you have made it through, in terms of the history of mathematics, to the seventeenth century. Number, measurement and geometry should now seem a little more exciting; you are becoming more confident in teaching these topics in a more inventive way using your mathematical eyes. The seventeenth century might seem a long time ago, but in terms of everyday common usage statistics, probability and algebra are relatively new. Statistics is all about cross-curricular working. Many subjects and businesses in our modern day world will use a statistical toolbox to inform, predict and present data. It's important for the children in your class to engage and enjoy this topic right from the start. If you think of topics in mathematics this is one they will all come across throughout their lives. So let's begin.

HISTORICAL BACKGROUND

The history of statistics dates back to a publication from 1663 called *Natural and Political Observations upon the Bills of*

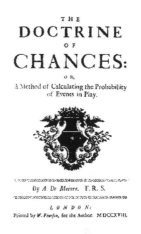

THE
DOCTRINE
OF
CHANCES:
OR,
A Method of Calculating the Probability
of Events in Play.

By *A. De Moivre*. F. R. S.

L O N D O N:
Printed by *W. Pearfon*, for the Author. M DCCXVIII.

FIGURE 6.1 Abraham de Moivre

Mortality written by John Graunt. His book looked at ways of collecting and analysing data on mortality.

Four years after the publication of Graunt's seminal work a French mathematician was born who was to change the way we think about probability – Abraham de Moivre.

His book, *The Doctrine of Chance*, published in 1718, was a great success, selling to a wide range of readers. Some of the people who bought his book were academics, as de Moivre was well known in English academic circles having been elected as a Fellow of the Royal Society of Mathematics. He was also a good friend of Sir Isaac Newton and through him met some of the greatest mathematicians of the time. His book was also very popular with gamblers, as they wished to know the correct way to play coin, dice and card games.

More later.

In the 1800s the mathematician Carl Friedrich Gauss was also involved in the initial formulation of statistics, carrying out a great deal of work on the concept of an average. He created a method to show the range of what is normally expected. This mathematical method is called the 'normal distribution'. His work with average is used today in many professions to test to see if things are normally average. For example when we are born our weight is taken to see if we fit the average pattern. If it is too low then additional tests are made. Another example of its use is seen when you take an IQ test and your result is ranked against what is normally expected.

CLASSROOM ACTIVITIES: STATISTICS

Statistics is the study of the collection, analysis and interpretation of data. Often, looking at data from experiments and surveys, statistics plays the important role of trying to make sense of large sets of numbers. Statistics is used in many different disciplines to interpret and make judgements about samples. It is a useful learning experience for children to collect small data samples and analyse these to see what they can find.

Average: mean

There are many different types of averages in a mathematical sense, but the most commonly used average, and the one used here, is called the 'arithmetic mean'. An average is a single number that can be used in place of a group of numbers. For example if I had three piles of coins with 24, 32 and 46 in each an average would smooth out these numbers and give a value of 34.

Although we don't have a pile of 34 coins in this instance (in our original three piles), the average number, 34, can be used as a representation of all three piles. You would find this value by adding up the three numbers to get 102 and then dividing by 3, as in this case there are three numbers.

We come across averages every day in the media. When talking about averages it's good to give real life examples to your class. For example we are often told about Mr Average in the press or on TV. He is married with two kids, has nine close pals, drinks three cups of tea and visits the loo six times a day. He has three tellies, reads Harry Potter and sleeps for about seven hours per night. But of course what this means is that there are people, lots of people, who drink more than three cups of tea a day and others who drink only one. The average takes away the large spread of numbers and leaves you with a single value, which hopefully gives a feel for what is happening.

Using stories to teach average

As you've seen in earlier chapters stories are a good way to introduce a topic to children. It's not only fun to read a story or poem to them: it also gives them a memory to recall when thinking about the topic in the future. The author A. A. Milne (1882–1956) is famous for his stories about Winnie the Pooh and Christopher Robin, Tigger and Piglet. His poem 'Halfway

Halfway down the stairs
is a stair
where I sit.
there isn't any
other stair
quite like
it.
I'm not at the bottom,
I'm not at the top;
so this is the stair
where
I always
stop.
Halfway up the stairs
Isn't up
And it isn't down.
It isn't in the nursery,
It isn't in town.
And all sorts of funny
thoughts
Run round my head.
It isn't really
Anywhere!
It's somewhere else
Instead!

FIGURE 6.2 Halfway down the stairs

Down . . . the stairs is a stair where I sit' can be used as a trigger for thinking about halfway distances. Once you've read the poem to the class ask them to get into groups of four. Two of the group stand a distance from each other and the third child has to guess (estimate) the halfway point between them. Then the fourth member of the group uses a tape measure to check the level of the accuracy of the estimation.

You can follow this activity by looking for other halfway points, such as using the width of the classroom, the length of the school corridor, the width of the school hall or the distance home from school.

It is also useful to ask children to think of the different ways they can find a halfway point for a given distance and the correct measuring equipment needed to do so. Children's suggestions may include a ruler, tape, trundle-wheel, non-standard units, feet, pacing out, human chains or a rope.

Human graphs

Using members of the class you can create human graphs and charts. These physical graphs give children a 'hands-on' experience of statistical representations. Let's look at how you can create a human bar chart in your classroom.

First, set the children a question in order to collect the data that will be used in the bar chart. An example could be:

What is your favourite colour?

Using rope/tape/ribbons create an X- and a Y-axis on the ground. Label the X-axis with the possible answers for their favourite colours – 'yellow', 'green', 'blue', 'red', etc. The students then stand (or lie down) in a line beside their favourite colour. Now label the Y-axis as 'Number of students'. You should now have a human bar chart. This will be the case if children are standing in the column by their favourite colour in the direction of the Y-axis.

From the bar chart the children will clearly be able to see which are the most and least popular colours. If you want them to work with this bar chart in more detail you could take an aerial type photo and display it. If the children have made their bar chart in the playground, taking a photo from a second floor window in the school would give a good vantage point.

You can also make human graphs for scatter plots, pictograms and line graphs.

Give it a go. It's great fun. The children will love it.

Once they have created their human graph ask them to reproduce this on graph paper in a more traditional form.

Here are a few ideas of the sorts of data you could collect to make your human graphs:

- the kinds of food in a packed lunch;
- the different ways of travelling to school;
- shoe sizes;
- the number of children in the family;
- birthday months or zodiac signs;
- the types of pets in the home;
- types of coats;
- favourite football teams.

Temperature and negative numbers

Collecting data on temperature is a natural way to introduce negative numbers. First let's take a look at the history of temperature so we have some background information to put the lesson in context for your class.

Daniel Gabriel Fahrenheit was born in Germany in 1686. He created the Fahrenheit temperature scale, which defines the freezing point of water as 32 degrees, with the boiling point as 212 degrees. In the twentieth century the Fahrenheit scale was replaced by the Celsius scale in most countries apart from the United States. The Fahrenheit and Celsius scales intersect at −40°. Therefore −40°F and −40°C represent the same temperature.

85

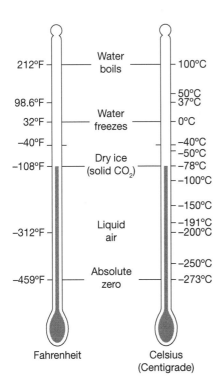

FIGURE 6.3 Temperature gauge

History of negative numbers

In the past, people believed negative numbers to be false because they could not see real world examples. They could have asked: how can you have a negative number of apples?

The earliest known use of negative numbers was in the book *Nine Chapters on the Mathematical Art* by Jiu-zhang Suanshu in 100 BC. Many years later in the seventh century, negative numbers were used as a method of representing debt in India. This is a very good example to use to think about negative numbers, even today. But as indicated above, temperature is a helpful real-life application for young children to grasp the concept.

Minus numbers, statistics and temperature

With young children the idea of 'not too hot, not too cold, just right', from the story of *Goldilocks and the Three Bears* leads naturally into a discussion about the experiences children have of temperature in their everyday life.

A nice activity is to ask the children to place photographs that show a range of different temperature environments and items (such as a bowl of soup, bathwater, a fire, a dishwasher, a kettle, a snowy day, a summer day, an iceberg, stepping into the swimming pool) onto a number line that has negative numbers. Creating concrete examples from their real memories helps them to think about the relative sizes of positive and negative numbers.

With children you can reinforce the idea of relative temperatures by talking about the temperature for your classroom. You could have a discussion about what temperature is just right or not for your classroom and ask your class to create tables, diagrams or human graphs of this data. This will help them to create memories of the temperature number line. You don't have to stop at your own classroom. Pose the question with your class:

Is the ideal temperature the same for all the rooms in the school?

By collecting real data on the temperature in different places around your school you can not only use this to sort and create graphical representations and then interpret your results, but also to think about wider issues such as: can your school be more energy efficient?

From this initial start you can easily create an investigation all about eco-issues around your school and the children's homes. You will then be teaching statistics through history, geography and current affairs. Here are a few questions to help you start thinking about this:

- How can you make your house/school more energy efficient?
- How did people keep warm down the centuries, and how do we do it today?
- What technologies can we add, both in our homes and in our community, that enable more efficient energy conservation?
- What are the most energy efficient materials from which to build a house?
- How do homes vary around the world owing to different climates?

We have looked at ways of collecting, sorting and analysing data; now let's move on to ways of analysing uncertainty with probability.

CLASSROOM ACTIVITY: PROBABILITY

Probability helps us to deal with our uncertain world. Being able to grasp the concept of probability allows children to make judgements about whether certain actions or events are more or less likely. Probability or risk is a measure regarding the likelihood of an event happening. A probability scale is a number line from 0 to 1 as shown in Figure 6.4.

I have always found that probability is a very useful topic to reinforce the concepts of fractions and decimals. Children need to think about the relative sizes of fractions and have conversations about these, for example that $\frac{1}{4}$ is smaller than $\frac{1}{2}$.

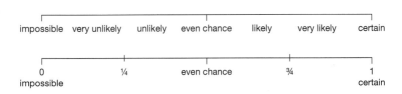

FIGURE 6.4 Probability scale

So if the probability of it raining today is $\frac{1}{4}$ then there is less chance of it raining than if the probability was $\frac{1}{2}$.

With the class you might like to think of some everyday examples when introducing probability. First, how about the weather? We get predictions about this every day in the media, often in terms of a percentage chance. Second, think about sports and games. Players of different sorts of games will look at the odds of winning and losing and therefore follow their most favourable strategies in order to improve their chance of success.

Let's take a look at probability with a physical activity, beginning with a simple flip of a coin. The children will probably already know there is a 50:50 chance of either flipping a head or a tail (with a fair coin). To obtain a rough experimental estimate of this chance, arrange your class in pairs and give one child one coin. Ask them to flip this coin and record the results. They need to work out the chance of them getting a head or a tail in their own ten flips.

Have a discussion about what they think will happen if they flip two coins. What are the different possibilities?

Now give each pair of children two coins that are different (e.g. a two pence and a ten pence coin) and repeat the flipping of a coin experiment, recording the four cases that can happen. When you flip two coins you get these possibilities: two heads (HH) or two tails (TT) or one head and one tail (HT) and one tail and one head (TH) (Table 6.1). Before de Moivre's time people were unsure about this, thinking that there were only three possibilities, counting HT and TH as the same.

TABLE 6.1 Probability for throwing two coins

		Second coin	
		H	T
First coin	H	HH	HT
	T	TH	TT

The chance of any one of these four cases is $\frac{1}{4}$. Once the children have performed this experiment you can discuss with them the chances that they have found. Remember it will not be obvious to a number of the children that there are four cases, so this is an important point to make clear.

You can guess what I'm going to suggest next: what happens with three coins? What are the possible outcomes in this case?

It is important to find out from the children what they think is going to happen when they flip three coins. Keep it a secret until the experiment is complete. It is best for children to discover results like this for themselves. They will be more likely to remember this in the future.

Here is a reminder so you know how to calculate the number of different ways in these sorts of coin experiments. If you have one coin there are two different outcomes that can occur: H or T. With two coins we have seen there are four different ways (2×2). For three coins there are eight ($2 \times 2 \times 2$) possible outcomes. When you flip four coins there are 16 ($2 \times 2 \times 2 \times 2$) possible outcomes, and so on.

Everyone has experience of random events. These could include the tossing of a coin at the start of a game of football, or the shuffling of cards, or weighing the risks and benefits of surgery. Most of us encounter chance daily and yet misconceptions abound. The psychologists Daniel Kahneman and Amos Tversky[1] suggest that generally people make decisions based on small sample sets, tending to reject randomness in the appearances of long runs in short samples, as they feel it seems too purposeful to be random.

For example in HTHTHHHHHHHHHH . . . what comes next?

People believe that after a long run of heads a tail is due, or maybe the next will be a head as heads are 'hot'. At its heart this gambler's fallacy lies in a misconception about fairness of the laws of chance. We believe chance to be a self-correcting process in which deviations in one direction will soon be countered with deviations in the other direction. In fact probability shows us that these deviations in the short run are not corrected. They are merely diluted over the long run.

Probability and the weather

Throughout this chapter we have been looking at ways of collecting and analysing data. Taking further these ideas and keeping the weather theme with your class you can record the weather over one week or longer if you like. Record your data for the weather patterns using statistical diagrams. Alongside your own data gathering keep a record on the predictions by the media and weathermen. They will give percentage probabilities for tomorrow's weather or on some devices hour by hour. You can then compare and look for how often the predicted weather turns out to be right and if the probability is a true reflection of what happens.

To add an inventive slant, how about using the St Swithun's Day weather rhyme or other weather related proverbs from the past. With the weather data you have collected you can check to see if any of these myths or proverbs or old wives' tales have any basis in scientific fact.

St Swithun, the Anglo Saxon bishop of Winchester of the eighth century, has a day named after him, which is 15 July. There is a weather rhyme linked to this day that goes like this:

St Swithun's day if thou dost rain
For forty days it will remain
St Swithun's day if thou be fair
For forty days 'twill rain nae mare.

Where this legend comes from is not clear, but many countries in Europe have similar proverbs about weather at this time of the year. France has three weather days on 8 June, 19 June and 6 July, and Germany has a 'Seven Sleepers Day' on 27 June. Germans believe that the weather on 27 June determines the average weather for the following seven weeks. Other weather related beliefs state that when a storm is coming flowers will close up and cows will lie down.

There are many weather related proverbs. Here are a few you may know:

- April showers bring May flowers.
- Red sky at night is a sailor's delight. Red sky in morning – sailor take warning.
- *If St Paul's day* [29 June] *be fair and clear,*
  it does betide a happy year.
  But if it chance to snow or rain,
  then will be dear all kinds of grain.
  If clouds or mists do dark the sky,
  great store of birds and beasts shall die.
  And if the winds do file aloft,
  then war shall vex the kingdom oft.
- *If Candlemas day* [2 February] *be dry and fair,*
  the half o' winters to come and mair.
  If Candlemas day be wet and foul,
  the half o' winter's gane at Yule.
- If you sneeze three times within a few seconds, the next day will be sunny.
- If it rains before seven, people say it will be fine for eleven.

MISCONCEPTIONS

When interpreting small samples from a large dataset children can sometimes make errors of judgement, believing that the sample truly represents all the data. Looking at sample data you should always ask your class to think about the wider issues when they come to interpretation or generalization.

NOTE

1 Kahneman and Tversky (1982).

Chapter 7

Almost there

Algebra

> Good teaching is one-fourth preparation and three-fourths theater.
> Gail Godwin

We set out at the start of this book on a journey, and as the title of this chapter suggests, we are almost there. At its roots mathematics is about spotting patterns. A mathematician could collect data and organize it. He or she would then look for general patterns in the data, trying to make sense of the whole. This would usually involve some abstraction into algebra. From these generalizations, on a good day, you would then be able to prove that the patterns you'd found were always true. Mathematics is a subject where you can prove a result is true beyond doubt. For some of your students the idea they can prove that something is always true will be the reason they love mathematics. So let's help them along the way and start to love algebra too. This chapter includes abstraction, expressions, equations, and substitution into formulae.

HISTORICAL BACKGROUND

The history of algebra starts over 4,000 years ago with the Egyptians and the Greeks, who were interested in expressing words as numbers, creating the idea of problems with 'unknown' numbers.

Al-Khwarizmi is credited with the invention of algebraic notational methods in AD 820. In his book *Al-jabr wa'l muqabalah* he sets out methods that follow a logical set of instructions to obtain the answer. This method he created we now call an algorithm, from the Latin corruption of his name, 'algorismus'.

It was not until the sixteenth century that the idea of algebraic methods really took hold and mathematicians started to solve equations using the rules of algebra that we use today. New symbols then started to appear with regularity in newly published papers. Today there are literally thousands of symbols in mathematical notation.

The word 'symbol' is derived from the ancient Greek word *Symbola*. The origins of this word come from the custom of breaking a clay tablet to mark a contract or agreement. Each piece identifies one of the people involved and it is only when all the pieces are joined together that you see the whole agreement. The word symbol has a sense of joining things together to create a whole that is greater than the sum of its parts. Many symbols used in mathematics are like this, as they represent abbreviated algebraic concepts.

Algebra and symbols are not just confined to the classroom. We constantly react to symbols in our everyday life. Using our mathematical eyes we see everyday symbols such as road signs that tell us to do something or give us information when we are using the roads.

Advertising symbols abound in the world we live. Companies hope that we will remember a jingle or catchphrase associated with their symbol and that this will persuade us to buy their product. Mathematical symbols are associated with certain quantities, operations and functions. These symbols can sometimes offer a memory aid, giving a clue as to how to use a particular mathematical technique. These abstract symbol quantities exist in our world and it is for this reason that we need children to be comfortable with algebra: to be able to deal with abstract quantities, use equations and to be able to substitute numbers into formulae.

FIGURE 7.1 Everyday symbols

The work of Ainley *et al.*[1] suggests that primary school children will benefit from time spent looking at ways of abstracting and representing patterns and symbols from real life situations.

So how can you make algebra more 'real' in your classroom? Lets take a look at a few possible ways of doing this and at the same time how you can build students' confidence in dealing with algebra.

CLASSROOM ACTIVITIES: ALGEBRA

What is algebra?

Over the last 400 years, algebra has underpinned our society's scientific and economic growth, as it gives us an ability to order patterns and predict the future.

One idea when starting to introduce algebra to your class is to bring along a present box and hide a number inside. Using a box and saying 'guess what number is inside the box?' is a more fun and less intimidating way of starting formal algebra.

So, set up your visual equation with the box and four bits of card (+, 6, =, 10) at the front of the class. You now have a visual way of showing the equation x + 6 = 10. Inside the box you will have hidden the number 4. You can think of the box as the unknown x. Therefore inside the box is the number your class have to find to make the sum work.

$$\text{🎁} + 6 = 10$$

FIGURE 7.2 x + 6 = 10

By using different numbers get the children used to the idea that the box (x) can take any value to make the sum work. You need to remember that if the equation has more than one x, each box has the same number hidden inside. In this more difficult example, you have two boxes plus seven on the left, equal to 25 minus the number in the box on the right. Each of the boxes are the same. They are all x and so they all have the same unknown value x.

$$\text{🎁} + \text{🎁} + 7 = 25 - \text{🎁}$$

FIGURE 7.3 x + x + 7 = 25 − x or 2x + 7 = 25 − x

In this puzzle you need to find the number in the box that gives the same answer on both sides of the equals sign. This hidden number in the box is a 6, as 2 times 6 plus 7 is 19, and 25 take away 6 is also 19.

Using two boxes of different colours you could solve equations with your children, such as the one shown in Figure 7.4.

+ **= 5**

FIGURE 7.4 $y + x = 5$

With this equation there are a range of answers, if you say to the children that the boxes need to contain whole positive numbers. These possible answers are 0 + 5, 1 + 4, 2 + 3, 3 + 2, 4 + 1, 5 + 0.

Richard Feynman, Physics Nobel Prize winner, said in his book *What Do You Care What Other People Think?*[2] that he used to watch his older cousin being taught algebra by a tutor. The tutor would ask, 'What is x in this equation?' His cousin would give the correct answer for x by arithmetic, and the tutor would say, 'Well that is right, but you didn't get it "by algebra"'. Feynman was never happy with this, as he maintained there was no such thing as solving 'by algebra', there was just solving. He said that when mathematicians are faced with algebraic equations that *no one has ever solved*, the first thing they do is to guess some values – to find the number in the box! Guessing the number in the box is a good place to start on the learning journey.

Of course once the children feel more comfortable guessing the number in the box you can start to teach them the rules of algebra. We will look at these rules later in the chapter. This will in the end make solving the equations easier, but only after students have grasped the initial concept of an unknown number being represented by a symbol (or a box).

Human pattern art

With young children the first step to learning algebra is to be able to abstract and use symbols: to take something from your world and to abstract it as a symbol. A nice game to play with young children to start this process is what I call 'human art'.

Divide your class into four by giving them a number from one to four. Each number relates to an action:

Number 1 – stand like a soldier;
Number 2 – stand like a star;
Number 3 – curl up like a ball;
Number 4 – stand like a tree.

Arrange the whole class to stand in a line in a repeating pattern such as 1, 2, 3, 4, 1, 2, 3, 4, 1, 2, 3, 4. Then ask the children to think of another repeating pattern they could create in their line such as 1, 1, 2, 2, 3, 3, 4, 4, 1, 1, 2, 2. Once they have tried this a few times ask the class to record the patterns they have made as a class on a piece of paper using symbols.[3]

Take some time to look at your students' work and see the level of abstraction they have in their symbols. The sorts of symbolic representation they use will vary greatly from one child to the next. Some may draw detailed pictures of the actions and others will represent a 'stand like a star' as an 'S'. This will give you a good starting point when you are thinking about your children's abstraction skills in the future. Let's now look to see how we can develop our skills to engage the class with a bit of maths magic.

CLASSROOM ACTIVITIES: ALGEBRAIC EXPRESSION AND MAGIC

Born in 1527 in England, John Dee lived in a different kind of academic world from the one we live in now. He was a mathematician, astronomer, astrologer, navigator and consultant to Queen Elizabeth I.

He spent much of his life studying the worlds of science, mathematics and magic. In his lifetime Dee amassed one of the largest libraries in England and his high status as a scholar also allowed him to play a role in Elizabethan politics. He gave talks on advanced algebra and was a leading expert in navigation.

Yet strange as it may seem today, in the last 30 years of his life Dee devoted much of his time to attempting to commune with angels in order to learn the universal language of creation. At the time Dee and others did not draw any distinction between mathematical research and investigations into magic and angel summoning. Instead they considered all of these activities to constitute different parts of the same quest in the search for a transcendental understanding of the divine form, which underlies the visible world. Dee called this quest of understanding the 'pure verities'.

Think of a number

Today a number of magicians use mathematics in their magic acts.[4] It is often misinterpreted that all magic involves sleight of hand, women being cut up into different fractional parts and rabbits hiding somewhere in a top hat. However, many magicians use a mathematical approach in order to create mind reading and prediction 'magic'. They practise for many hours a day to get their maths magic right, looking smooth and professional. When you do this activity with your class you can tell them not to worry if they don't get their 'performance' right the first time, as practise makes perfect.

First let's look at two examples for you to think about the concept. Give this one a go yourself and see the magic unfold.

TABLE 7.1 Think of a number – No. 1

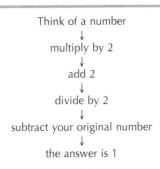

Think of a number
↓
multiply by 2
↓
add 2
↓
divide by 2
↓
subtract your original number
↓
the answer is 1

It's obviously not magic. The idea is set out in this algebra chapter and is not being sold in a magic shop! How does it work? You'll need to know, as in your inventive algebra lesson you'll be explaining to the class how your children can become 'algebra magicians'.

Let's go through the trick with the algebra beside each step, as shown in Table 7.2.

TABLE 7.2 Think of a number – No. 1 – answer

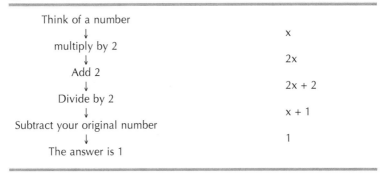

Think of a number	
↓	x
multiply by 2	
↓	2x
Add 2	
↓	2x + 2
Divide by 2	
↓	x + 1
Subtract your original number	
↓	1
The answer is 1	

Let's look at one more illustration, similar to the one above, before moving on to how you can use this in your algebra class. Table 7.3 gives a different think of a number trick with algebra beside each step.

TABLE 7.3 Think of a number – No. 2 – answer

Think of a number	
↓	x
Double it	
↓	2x
Add 9	
↓	2x + 9
Add the original number	
↓	3x + 9
Divide by 3	
↓	x + 3
Add 7	
↓	x + 10
Subtract the original number	
↓	10
The answer is 10	

You are now ready to 'perform' these two think of a number algebra examples to the class as mind reading magic. If you want to add more 'colour' you can use number cards or dice to generate the starting number. What I mean by this is you would ask the student to think of a number by throwing dice or picking a number card.

There are two parts to this classroom activity. First the children are required to determine how the think of a number algebra works. So provide them with an illustration, such as in Tables 7.2 and 7.3, with x as the unknown number. This part shows the practicality of abstracting in algebra. Second, challenge them to develop their own think of a number magic algebra performance. This usually works best in pairs. Towards the end of the lesson children can come out to the front and give their magic performance. Again this is to trigger those 'emotionally' strong memories about their algebra lesson. By giving and taking part in a magic performance makes algebra seem more accessible and comprehensible.

Pick two cards, any cards

A more advanced version of think of a number involves place value. To do this activity you'll need a pack of playing cards.[5] Take out the hearts and spades numbered one to nine. Taking on the role of the magician in your class, ask a spectator (a child) to pick one heart and one spade, without you seeing which ones they have chosen. Then ask them to follow the instructions in Table 7.4, without disclosing any of the answers.

TABLE 7.4 Pick a card

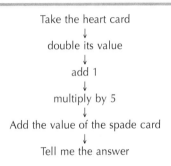

Take the heart card
↓
double its value
↓
add 1
↓
multiply by 5
↓
Add the value of the spade card
↓
Tell me the answer

For example if the spectator picked the 4 of hearts and 7 of spades, he or she would have doubled the 4 to get 8, then added 1 to get 9 and multiplied by 5 to get 45. Finally, by adding 7 (the spade value), a total of 52 is reached.

When you are told the final answer, in your head, always subtract 5. The number you have will show you the two card values. In this case 52 take 5 is 47. You can give the answer of the 4 of hearts and the 7 of spades.

Looking at the algebra shows how this trick works and also lets you make your own personal tricks.

Let's say the red heart card is R and the black spade card is B.

TABLE 7.5 Pick a card algebra

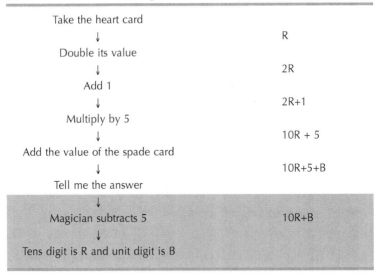

Take the heart card	R
↓	
Double its value	2R
↓	
Add 1	2R+1
↓	
Multiply by 5	10R + 5
↓	
Add the value of the spade card	10R+5+B
↓	
Tell me the answer	
↓	
Magician subtracts 5	10R+B
↓	
Tens digit is R and unit digit is B	

As in the 'think of a number' activity, now see if you can create your own maths magic variations of the above tricks. Your class will love to try and create their own magic as well. This sort of activity, as I have already stated, is very empowering as children are creating their own mathematics.

CLASSROOM ACTIVITIES: ALGEBRA EQUATIONS

Consequences game: 'topsy turvy' algebra

The traditional game of consequences is played using a piece of paper with one person writing words without others seeing and then folding the paper to hide the words. They then pass the paper to the next person who adds their own words in secret, folds and passes on. This continues until the paper is completely folded and no more words can be added.

The consequence game format can be adapted to develop confidence with equations, giving children the opportunity to see how equations can be manipulated and developed. Let me illustrate how this activity can be used in the classroom.

The children work in pairs. One child starts by writing the value of 'x' at the top of the page without the other child seeing. Under this they then write an equivalent equation by performing the same operation to both sides. This operation, for example, might be multiplying both sides by 2, or adding 3 to each side. They fold the paper so their partner can only see the second equation. They pass the paper over for their partner to perform another operation to both sides. They then fold the paper so now only their equation can be seen. This procedure is repeated. I have found that the number of 'repeats' is often linked to the confidence and ability of the children with algebra. So, start by just doing one fold repeat, though after practice the children may be able to continue repeating until the paper is full.

Once the game is finished the paper is opened up so that both players can now see all of the steps that have been made. What they will see (if they have not made any mistakes) is a solution to the equation at the bottom of the page, thus creating an 'upside down' 'topsy turvy' solution, starting with the answer and creating the question. Still in their pairs, the children can look at the whole solution and take the initial value for x and put it in the final equation to check and make sure the equation is valid and they have not made any errors during the process.

103

TABLE 7.6 The consequences game

Step 1:	Step 2:	Step 3:	Step 4:	Step 5:
x = 2 3x = 6	Fold and hide 3x = 6	Fold and hide 3x + 5 = 11	Uncover all steps x = 2 3x = 6 3x + 5 = 11	Check answer by substitution of x = 2 into the final equation and work backward.

If they find it is not correct they need to locate the mistake. Again this is a good stage in developing algebraic appreciation. Once any errors have been spotted and corrected they both need to be able to explain to the other how they each manipulated each side and ended up with the final equation. The operation used at each stage can be annotated on their final solution.

x = 2.

The player may multiply both sides by 3:

3x = 2 × 3

and write 3x = 6 on the paper and fold this so the next player cannot see x = 2.

The next student may add 5 to both sides:

3x + 5 = 6 + 5

and write 3x + 5 = 11 on the paper.

At this point the next student has to try and work out what x is equal to by working backwards, i.e. subtract 5 from both sides and divide by 3.

Practising in this way with topsy turvy algebra helps students understand why we need to perform certain operations when solving equations; and, due to its informal (fun) setting, it also builds children's confidence in dealing with algebraic manipulations.

Formulas in geometry

Leonhard Euler was a Swiss mathematician born in the early eighteenth century. He is known as the 'King of Mathematics' as he has published more pieces of mathematical work than anyone else who has ever lived. He is also my favourite mathematician.

Who is yours?

Do your students have a favourite mathematician?

How many mathematicians can they name?

The final activity in this chapter is about substitution into a formula. I have chosen to look at the amazing formula $F + V - E = 2$ created by Euler, which always gives an answer of 2. Euler's genius gave him the insight to be able to show that all shapes have common features. By counting the faces (F), vertices (V) and edges (E) of a shape the formula shows the answer will always be the constant value of 2 no matter which shape you have chosen.

Euler.

FIGURE 7.5 Leonhard Euler

Taking a cube as an example let's try Euler's formula. A cube has 6 faces, 8 vertices and 12 edges, so substituting these numbers into the formula we get:

$$6 + 8 - 12 = 2$$

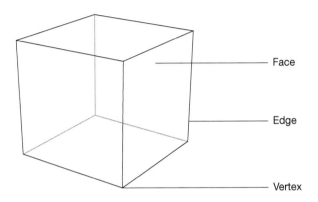

Face

Edge

Vertex

FIGURE 7.6 Cube

With the class you can use Euler's formula to look at a range of 2D and 3D shapes. First, ask the children to name as many 2D and 3D shapes as they can. Second, in groups they can record the number of faces, edges and vertices for specific shapes the class is looking at as part of their shape activities.

TABLE 7.7 Shapes and Euler's formula

Name	Image	Faces F	Vertices V	Edges E	Euler characteristics $F + V - E$
Tetrahedron		4	4	6	2
Cube		6	8	12	2
Octahedron		8	6	12	2
Dodecahedron		12	20	30	2
Icosahedron		20	12	30	2

The children could make and design a poster celebrating the work of the great Leonhard Euler or their 'favourite' mathematician.

MISCONCEPTIONS

Some children find it difficult to accept the use of letters as unknown numbers. They are likely to require a great deal of practice expressing statements in words before thinking of abstracting these as numbers, signs and letters.

NOTES

1 Ainley *et al.* (2009).
2 Feynman (2007).
3 Hart *et al.*'s (1989) work highlights the difficulties many children have moving from pictorial representations to symbolic ones and how worthwhile it is to spend time in class supporting this from an early age.
4 Fulves (1983) gives a great range of number tricks that can be used in lessons.
5 Scarne was one of the greatest mathematical magicians. His book contains 155 self-working tricks that give the opportunity to engage in the beauty of algebra (see Scarne 1950).

Chapter 8

Starting your own new journey

> One cannot tell anyone anything unless they are ready to hear it.
>
> Godbole in the film script of *A Passage to India*
> by E.M. Forster (1924)

Having been an educationalist for over 29 years I've seen that children being engaged in creative mathematical activities can embed and motivate learning. Not only is this true in school, when actively involved in the lesson, but it also overlaps into their personal time at home. I've had many children come back the next day after experiencing maths taught in an inventive way and say 'Sir, look what I have found while I was working on this at home'. Motivating learning is one of the keys to creating a positive experience for all learners. It was not until I came across research that looked at the benefits of 'transfer triggers' that I realized that my approach to teaching mathematics using real world examples and allowing children to use their mathematical eyes really was the way to go. The other element that my experience has shown me to be of great value regarding children's mathematical memory is emotion.

I remember being in class one day when Peter, one of my students, told me about his idea of speeding up a calculation for an activity I had set. Peter said 'Sir, I've found a quicker way to get the answer, could you look at it?' Peter struggled in class and I had assumed that he did not enjoy his maths lessons. Yet while he was telling me his idea he was excited about his discovery. His method was simple, but good. I asked him to relay his theory to the class, but he asked me to do this and I did. I called his idea 'Peter's method'. The class thought it was great and everyone used it. After that day Peter changed and so did I; his maths improved greatly and I would never assume again. Throughout the rest of the year the class would sometimes say to him 'Peter, have you got a quick method for this one?' He would reply, 'I'm working on it.' And I believed he was.

BELIEFS

Few would argue that the beliefs we hold as teachers influence our perceptions and judgements, which in turn affect our behaviour in the classroom. Thinking about why we teach in a certain way is essential to improving our own teaching practices. Research has shown this to be true.[1] Teachers often transfer their own beliefs to their students. The way in which they teach is often built upon a variety of experiences based on their own learning – typically at school or through observations of lessons while in initial teacher training.[2] Because they learnt in one particular way, giving them one limited snapshot of learning, this leads teachers to believe that delivering similar types of lessons will allow their students to achieve as they did.

If teachers have experienced failure in classrooms which were harsh with strict discipline, then they will be inclined to believe that friendly fun activities may provide a more positive environment in which to learn. Alternatively if organized structure is a strong classroom memory from the teacher's youth this belief may influence the way in which he or she teaches. If in their own educational settings the teacher learnt mathematical concepts successfully by rote or memorization they will believe that this is the way to teach certain mathematical topics. When their own pupils misunderstand the concept owing to rote learning and therefore make errors, the teacher will interpret this as carelessness or lack of attention.

Taking one's own beliefs from a small snapshot of schooling could be said to be similar to looking at a very small sample of student outcomes taken from a large distribution and assuming the very small sample is representative. If the small sample is made up of gifted children scoring very high marks then it would be assumed that the whole sample would also score high marks. So my point is that basing one's own teaching practice on one's own experience can be limiting.

Research shows that 'teachers' beliefs about themselves, about mathematics, about teaching, and about their students shape what they do in the classroom'.[3] There are no clear logical rules for determining a person's belief. One belief can be a mixture of personal and emotional experiences. A teacher's belief will often be reinforced by positive feedback from their students. Often teachers do not hold these beliefs consciously, that is they don't know they have them. This can make it difficult for a teacher to reflect on and change their own practice.

There are four major types of 'belief' systems.[4]

Existential beliefs – In terms of teaching this is the idea of the existence of a teacher's belief in the ability, maturity and consciousness of students. These are not just labels a teacher assigns to students and classes but how a teacher categorizes groups of students and hence structures the learning given to the class. These types of beliefs make teachers think that students who fail to learn do so because they do not work hard enough. The teacher's belief is that the way to do well in class is to do extra work and practise more. Alternatively if the existential teacher's belief is that maturity is the key to learning then treating students as adults and allowing them to organize their own learning would create classroom structures that involve discussion. In doing this, these teachers are taking some very abstract human characteristics and creating concrete entities as a way of bringing these characteristics under their control and influence.

Alternativity beliefs – Belief structures often include the idea of alternative realities, for example some sort of ideal world such as a utopian society. In school classroom contexts this manifests itself in a teacher trying to create an environment that is based on some abstract model they have heard about but never seen in practice. The teachers who have these beliefs are undaunted by setbacks as they see themselves on a journey to reach their special classroom.

Affective and evaluative beliefs – Feelings, moods and subjective evaluations based on personal preferences can be easily distinguished from knowledge about a particular concept. The amount of energy a teacher will give to a particular aspect of teaching will be determined by the teacher's personal preferences. This will also be an important factor when it comes to thinking about teachers' conceptions of a particular subject matter. These kinds of beliefs are also important when you think about the consequences of a teacher's feelings about different students in the class.

Episodic beliefs – Research shows that knowledge is stored primarily in semantic structural networks, while belief systems are episodically stored in personal experiences, episodes or events.

Effective teaching, according to research, is based on a set of beliefs and a collection of subject knowledge.[5] However, belief systems are relatively static compared with a person's knowledge. Therefore when a belief actually does change it is likely to be a monumental shift in that person's point of view.

Reflecting on your own beliefs

After reading about different types of beliefs, you need now to sit back and think about what your own specific beliefs about teaching are. Think of something in teaching that you are passionate about and firmly believe in. This may seem like a difficult question to answer, but it takes you to the very heart of why you teach the way you do. Ask yourself: if someone were observing my class, what in my teaching behaviour would reflect this passion? Why do I do this?

Why do I teach the way I do?

EMOTION

It has been found that by increasing rehearsal, enhancing attention and increasing elaboration there is a stimulation of memory advantage alongside emotional stimuli.[6]

Modifying a hypothesis from neuroscience provides us with some explanation as to why providing children with learning experiences that stimulate emotional participation can lead to a longer-term memory recall. Figure 8.1 provides a starting point. Following the arrows shows us that the lesson that stimulates a child allows them to interpret meaning. This incites a cognitive emotional response, which then influences memory storage in the long term and influences coping behaviour in the short run.

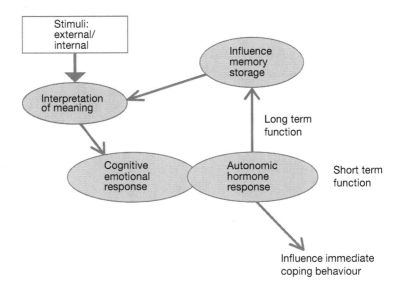

FIGURE 8.1 Memory and the adaptive role in the response to future situations

Source: Modified from Cahill and McGaugh (1998)

Throughout this book I have demonstrated a series of class-room activities that are designed to trigger an emotional response to learning. I have found during my teaching career that these kinds of activities help to support children's long term memories regarding mathematical concepts. But it's not all about memory. It's about giving children confidence and a willingness to try. It's also about explaining mathematical ideas from an inventive perspective that encourages children to take part, think about maths differently and associate what they are learning with their everyday lives.

THE JOURNEY IN THIS BOOK

Throughout the book I've used a range of different inventive ideas to create classroom activities. We started the journey switching on your mathematical eyes, making you aware that we all live in a mathematical world. I have shown in Chapter 1 how to plan, organize and carry out a maths walk with your class. But this was not only about creating a maths walk but about seeing how mathematics can be taught from a new and different perspective. For instance, you may not have realized or considered that you live in a mathematical world where architects are using Euclid's shapes, that farmers divide up their land in the same way as the Ancient Egyptians did, and that we are living on Babylonian time? Over the next six chapters I then proceeded to look at the main topics featured in primary mathematics. Starting with number, I endeavoured to provide you with a fresh look at number patterns, fractions and decimals using historical stories, magic, games, puzzles and other original activities. Maybe you remember Audrey Hepburn's destiny number or what $\frac{1}{7}$ looks like on your calculator as a repeating pattern. The journey continued with our meeting dinosaurs, the Abominable Snowman, Peter Rabbit and the animals in the Chinese zodiac – all to help children relate to measurement. For geometry we took children on an imaginative journey to the supermarket and to an art gallery so as to re-open their mathematical eyes with a colourful look at shape. They became 'shape detectives' as well as eco-friendly investigators. It's often said that the British are preoccupied by the weather. So in the chapter looking at statistics and probability we took a quirky look at proverbs and old wives' tales to examine weather conditions and their predictions. Organizing your first human graph outside in the playground will probably be something you'll always remember and so will your students. The final topic was the 'grammar' of mathematics. With number presents hidden in boxes, children taking the role of algebra magicians and meeting the great Leonhard Euler, algebra can now be taught in an exciting and colourful way.

ROAD MAP FOR THE FUTURE

Having worked your way through this guide I hope that I have provided you with tools that you can use to become a more inventive mathematics teacher. Hopefully, you'll be able to create some new ideas of your own using the blueprint that accompanies each of the topics. This guide will help to provide you with the confidence and belief that you can be just as creative in your lessons. I hope that your future maths teaching journey is interesting, colourful and varied. Remember your journey has only just begun and to help you get started I suggest that you try developing the mathematical ideas in the book and the Appendix, remembering all the different tools we have looked at.

NOTES

1 For the place of teachers' beliefs in research on teacher thinking and decision making, and for an alternative methodology, see Munby (1982); for the role of beliefs in the practice of teaching see Nespor (1987).
2 Eddy (1969).
3 Schoenfeld (2011), p. 26.
4 Schank and Abelson (1977).
5 Askew *et al.* (1997).
6 McGaugh *et al.* (2000). Section 11

Ten more starting points to help you become an inventive primary mathematics teacher

In this appendix you will find a set of mathematical starting points for you to use in order to start to develop your own outstanding lessons. When putting together your lesson remember to use all your newly developed skills such as switching on the children's mathematical eyes and thinking how you are going to create that episodic learning to stimulate their memory. Ask yourself: what triggers can I use in the lesson that will allow the children to build on previous memories?

When you are starting to develop a new lesson you should always begin with the key mathematical concept that you are trying to teach. You will need to think about which point in the lesson will be most appropriate to introduce this to the class. When this time comes in the lesson don't waste that moment. Think carefully beforehand about what you are going to say and the language you are going to use. Perhaps for the first few lessons you create write out a small script so you can think carefully about the point you are trying to get across. This key moment of conversation in the lesson will be over in a few seconds, but if you get it right it will latch onto the child's memory. The lesson will have been a colourful, memorable episode, creating a strong memory on which to place this key kernel of a mathematical idea. Over time you will see your children progress with greater confidence. A good teacher says very little in a class. The few key words they do say are enough for the children to take their own understanding further.

1 BENFORD'S LAW

Benford's Law states that in a list of numbers, such as electricity bills, stock prices, population numbers, death rates, lengths of rivers and mathematical constants, the chance of the first digit being a 1 is about 30%. Larger digits appear in this first position with lower and lower frequency; for example 9 as a first digit occurs only 4.6% of the time. The graph in Figure A.1 shows the chances for each number from 1 to 9. So for 6 the chance would be 6.7%.

This result is named after physicist Frank Benford, who first discussed this concept in a paper he wrote in 1938.

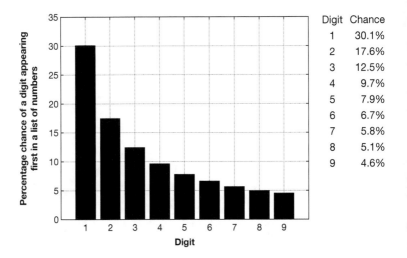

Digit	Chance
1	30.1%
2	17.6%
3	12.5%
4	9.7%
5	7.9%
6	6.7%
7	5.8%
8	5.1%
9	4.6%

FIGURE A.1 Benford's Law

This curious finding might make you wonder and want to do your own checks to validate Benford's result. A good place to start would be to look at the FTSE 100 stock prices.

Which areas of mathematical learning would you develop by using Benford's Law?

2 PATTERNS IN THE PRIMES

A number which can only be divided by itself and 1 without a remainder is called a prime number. Mathematicians have been searching for patterns in prime numbers for over 3,000 years and have made only a small amount of progress, believing that there are still many patterns to find. Figure A.2 shows a spiral of the first 48 numbers with the primes shaded.

42	43	44	45	46	47	48
41	20	21	22	23	24	25
40	19	6	7	8	9	26
39	18	5	0	1	10	27
38	17	4	3	2	11	28
37	16	15	14	13	12	29
36	35	34	33	32	31	30

FIGURE A.2 Patterns in the primes

This is a list of the primes that are less than 100:

2, 3, 5, 7, 11, 13, 17, 19, 23, 29, 31, 37, 41, 43, 47, 53, 59, 61, 67, 71, 73, 79, 83, 89, 97

You could start by creating a hundred prime spiral grid and asking the children to see what patterns can be found. These could be number or shape patterns. What patterns can you see?

What is the key piece of mathematics for which you are using the primes as a learning tool: primes, factors, special numbers, patterns, cross-curricula art maths?

3 THE GOLDEN RATIO

If you join up the diagonals of a regular pentagon you will create a five-pointed star with a pentagon at its centre. These pentagons are linked to each other by something that the Greeks named the golden ratio (see Figure A.3). The ratio of the sides of these pentagons will always be 1.618 . . .

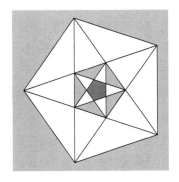
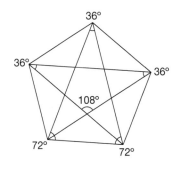

FIGURE A.3 The golden ratio

The golden ratio appears in many growth patterns in plants and animals, such as the nautilus shell, starfish, stems and branches of plants, veins of leaves, to name but a few.

The Greeks built their statues in this ratio as they felt it was pleasing to the eye. In the fifteenth century Luca Pacioli wrote and Leonardo da Vinci illustrated the best selling book *De Divina Proportione*, which captured the imagination of artists and architects for centuries. The so-called 'rule of thirds' is still often mentioned today in photography as a way of setting up a well-proportioned picture. It is called the rule of thirds as $\frac{5}{3}$ is approximately the golden ratio.

Think about how you could use the golden ratio using the children's faces and bodies for working on measurement, accuracy, ratio and proportion.

4 THE NUMBER FOUR

Surprisingly, four is the only number in the English language 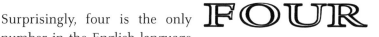 that contains the same number of letters as its name. You may think that mathematically this is not of any great interest but you can use this fact to play this interesting number game.

Choose any number whatsoever, write it down as a word, count the number of letters and use this value to name a new number. Count the number of letters in the new number and use this to name the next number, and so on.

No matter what number you start with, you will eventually end up with four.

For example if we start with TEN, we can note that there are 3 letters in this word. The word THREE has 5 letters, so this means you get the word FIVE. The word FIVE has 4 letters and hence we have ended up with FOUR!

Start with TWENTY (six letters).
We get SIX (three letters).
We now have THREE (five letters).
We now have FIVE
... and once again we end up with FOUR!

Does this idea work in other languages? Can you use this mathematical idea to create cross-curricula learning? Is there a range of mathematical skills that this idea can help develop? Does this idea make you ask: why does it work and will it always work for any number?

5 CALCULATING CAN BE FUN

If you use eight 8s together, as below, you get one thousand:

$$\frac{8888 - 888}{8} = 1000$$

$$\left(\frac{88 - 8}{0.8}\right) \times \left(8 + \frac{8 + 8}{8}\right) = 1000$$

Sets of eights have some curious number properties such as the pattern in this calculation:

$$12345679 \times 8 = 98765432$$

Or what about taking the nine digits 1–9 in order and remove the 8, then multiply this number by 9 and you get nine 1s:

$$12345679 \times 9 = 111111111$$

Multiplying sets of 9s together creates number patterns only involving 9, 8, 1 and 0 as you can see below:

$$9 \times 9 = 81$$

$$999 \times 999 = 998001$$

I have given you just a few quirky number calculations to get you started. You could ask the children to find more. Exploring the world of number enables children to become more confident not only with calculations and calculators but also with the surprising world of mathematics.

6 PATTERNS EVERYWHERE

Starting with three different randomly placed colours on a top row of ten, a correct prediction can always be made about the colour of the final resulting colour at the bottom of the triangle by looking at the first and last colours in this first row.

Let me show you how to do this.

First you will need at least 55 pieces of card made up of three colours – in this example we have yellow (Y), blue (B) and red (R). Place ten cards of random colours on the top row. The rule for creating the second row is to look at the row above:

- if two consecutive colours in the row above are the same, then place the same colour in between them in the next row;
- if the two consecutive colours in the row above are different then place the third colour in between them in the next row.

This process needs to continue building rows of 9, 8, 7, etc. until the whole triangle, such as is seen in Figure A.4, is formed.[1]

FIGURE A.4 Triangle pattern with ten start

The curiosity of this pattern is that from the top row you can identify the final colour of the piece of card at the bottom of the triangle. Look at the first and last entries on the top row: they are yellow and blue in the example above. By following the same rules that you used to build the triangle you know that the final entries at the bottom of the triangle will be red.

FIGURE A.5 Triangle patterns with four start

Starting with a top row of four you could ask the children to experiment. What patterns can they find in this piece of mathematical art? What happens if they change the rules and invent their own mathematical art patterns?

NOTE

1 A 2013 paper by Behrends and Humble gives the full mathematical background to this amazing pattern.

7 THE PERSISTENCE OF ANY NUMBER

The persistence of any number is defined as the number of times you need to multiply its digits together before you reach a single digit.

For example with 246 when you multiply the digits together you get $2 \times 4 \times 6 = 48$. Then 48 is 4×8, which gives 32, and then multiplying 3 by 2 you get 6. This gives the persistence of 246 as three, as it took three steps to reduce the number to a single digit.

Here is another example. 39 is the smallest number known which takes three steps to reduce it to a single digit. $39 \rightarrow 27 \rightarrow 14 \rightarrow 4$. Any number smaller than 39 will have a persistence of two or one. Table A.1 shows the smallest numbers for any given persistence value.

TABLE A.1 Persistence table

Persistence	Smallest number
1	10
2	25
3	39
4	77
5	679
6	6788
7	68889
8	2677889
9	26888999
10	3778888999
11	277777788888899

It is thought that no number has persistence more than 11, but this has as yet not been proven. Maybe a challenge for the future mathematicians in your class.

This idea could be used in a lesson on number and multiplying or you could be more creative and involve number sequence journeys. How would you encourage the children to find systematically different persistence sequences?

8 PEOPLE AND THEIR NUMBERS

Niven numbers

Born in 1915, Ivan Niven was a Canadian–American mathematician who specialized in number theory. Niven numbers are named after him.

A Niven number is a whole number that is divisible by the sum of its digits. For example take the number 24. If you add the digits this gives 2 + 4 = 6, and 6 divides exactly into 24, four times.

The first few Niven numbers are 10, 12, 18, 20, 21, 24, 27, 30, 36, 40, 42, 45, 48, 50, 54, 60, 63, 70, 72, 80, 81, 84, 90, 100 . . .

Smith numbers

An example of a Smith number is 27. You can see that the sum of the digits of 27 is 2 + 7, which equals 9. With Smith numbers this value of 9 is the same as the sum of the digits of 27's prime factors: 3 + 3 + 3.

Another Smith number is 58. The reason 58 is also a Smith number is that when you add the digits 5 + 8 you get 13. Adding the digits of 58's prime factors (2 × 29 = 58) you can see that 2 + 9 + 2 also equals 13.

Smith numbers were only discovered recently in 1982 when university mathematician Albert Wilansky saw that his brother-in-law's phone number had this strange property. The phone number was 493-7775 and has prime factors of 3 × 5 × 5 × 65837. When you add these digits and the digits in the phone number you get 42. You guessed it, 4,937,775 is a Smith number.

Wilansky was so surprised by this result that he named it after his brother-in-law Harold Smith.

The first few Smith numbers are:

4, 22, 27, 58, 85, 94, 121, 166, 202, 265, 274, 319, 346, 355, 378, 382, 391, 438, 454, 483, 517, 526, 535, 562, 576, 588, 627, 634, 636, 645, 648, 654, 663, 666, 690, 706, 728, 729, 762, 778, 825, 852, 861, 895, 913, 915, 922, 958, 985.

Two consecutive Smith numbers such as 728 and 729 are called Smith brothers.

There are many 'named' numbers creating opportunities for you to think about different ways for the children to learn facts about numbers. In lessons on calculation, factors and pattern you could explore with your children the world of named numbers and discover curious mathematicians who inhabit that world.

9 UNLUCKY NUMBERS

Good and bad superstitions about numbers have developed alongside the cultural growth of civilizations and continue to do so. Some of these number superstitions were thought to help ward off danger or summon good fortune. Amulets would have been made with lucky numbers or magic squares engraved on them. From these early superstitions grew many curious customs, which still remain to the present day. The superstition that 13 is unlucky results in some hotels and office buildings not having rooms or floors labelled 13. The most popular explanation for 13 being unlucky is that at the Last Supper there was Jesus and the 12 Apostles, with the 13th guest being Judas Iscariot who went on to betray Jesus. This superstition continues today. When people know there are 13 guests coming for dinner they often take a soft toy/teddy bear to take the 14th seat.

The fear of the number 17 is called 'heptadecaphobia'.

In Italy the number 17 is considered unlucky just as 13 has the superstition of being unlucky in other cultures. The Roman numeral for 17 is written as XVII with X as 10, V as 5 and I as 1. When this numeral is rearranged it spells out 'VIXI', which in Latin means 'I have lived'. Some people think that this gave rise to the unlucky superstition as it could imply 'My life is over'. Note that when you are adding Roman numerals you would write VI + XI = 6 + 11 = 17.

BUT it's not all sad.

A happy number is defined in the following way. Start with any positive whole number, square its digits and then add the result. Repeat this process until the answer you get equals 1, or the answer loops endlessly in a cycle which does not include 1.

Those numbers for which this process ends in 1 are called 'happy numbers', while those that do not end in 1 are 'unhappy numbers' or 'sad numbers'.

For example, 19 is said to be happy since

$1^2 + 9^2 = 82$
$8^2 + 2^2 = 68$
$6^2 + 8^2 = 100$
$1^2 + 0^2 + 0^2 = 1$.

The first few happy numbers are:

1, 7, 10, 13, 19, 23, 28, 31, 32, 44, 49, 68, 70, 79, 82, 86, 91, 94, 97, 100, 103, 109, 129, 130, 133, 139, 167, 176, 188, 190, 192, 193, 203, 208, 219, 226, 230, 236, 239, 262, 263, 280, 291, 293, 301, 302, 310, 313

Do numbers trigger emotions for the children in your class? You could make a wall display looking at happy and sad numbers, with the children finding out facts about their favourite numbers.

10 MATHEMATICAL DOODLING: KOBON TRIANGLE PUZZLE

What is the largest number of non-overlapping triangles that can be created by drawing a set of straight lines? With three lines the most you can make is one triangle (Figure A.6).

FIGURE A.6 Three-line triangle

With four lines you can create two triangles, with five lines you can create five triangles and with six lines you can create seven triangles (Figure A.7).

FIGURE A.7 Four-, five- and six-line triangles

As you can see from Figure A.8, if you keep drawing in a new line it gets more and more complex to find the maximum number of possible triangles you can create. This is called the Kobon triangle puzzle.

FIGURE A.8 Kobon triangle puzzle

The general formula for how many triangles you get, given any number of lines, has not yet been discovered. Some of the known results are shown in Table A.2.

TABLE A.2 Kobon triangle

Number of lines	3	4	5	6	7	8	9	10	11
Maximum number of triangles	1	2	5	7	11	15	21	25	32

What shapes other than triangles can be named and identified in the Kobon patterns? If your key focus is to learn about triangles you could use Kobon to trigger questions about the number of different kinds of triangles that can be found.

What happens if you create quadrilaterals instead of triangles?

Glossary

A selection of useful words to add to your mathematical vocabulary.

acute angle: an angle between 0° and 90°.

algorithm: a set of predefined steps that produce a correct result when performing a calculation.

associative law of addition: the principle that if three numbers are added, the order in which this addition is carried out makes no difference, i.e. (a + b) + c = a + (b + c).

base 10: our base ten system has the ten digits (0 to 9) and this is why powers of ten are used in the place value system: 1000, 100, 10, 1, 0.1, 0.01, 0.001.

capacity: how much liquid volume a container can hold when full.

cardinal number: the concept that a number has meaning representing a set of positive objects, e.g. 5 apples.

circumference: the special name given to the perimeter of a circle.

commutative law of multiplication: the principle that the order of a multiplication calculation makes no difference. For example $3 \times 4 = 4 \times 3$ and $a \times b = b \times a$.

congruent shapes: two plane or solid figures that have the same shape and size.

conjecture: a hypothesis, something that has been deduced from existing facts.

cube: a cuboid with all square faces.

cube number: a number that is obtained by multiplying a whole number by itself three times. Here are the first few cube numbers 1, 8, 27, 64, . . .

cuboid: a rectangular prism in which any two opposite faces are identical rectangles.

cyclic decimal: a decimal where one or more of the digits after the decimal point repeats forever, for example 0.123123123123 . . . .

denominator: the bottom number of a fraction. The denominator is the total number of parts.

digits: these are the numerals: 0, 1, 2, 3, 4, 5, 6, 7, 8, 9.

edge: the straight line that joins a polygon or the line edge where two plane surfaces meet in a 3D solid.

empty number line: this is a number line without a scale.

equilateral triangle: a triangle with all three sides equal in length; three angles each equal to 60°.

equivalent fraction: two or more fractions that represent the same fraction. For example $\frac{1}{2} = \frac{3}{6}$

face: the shape that is bounded by the edges on a 3D object.

factor: a number that divides another number exactly leaving no remainder.

heptagon: a seven-sided polygon.

hexagon: a six-sided polygon. 'Hex' means 'six'.

improper fraction: a fraction in which the numerator is greater than the denominator, e.g. $\frac{8}{5}$.

inequality: a mathematical statement that one number is greater than another (>) or less than another (<). For example 23 > 18 and 45 < 48.

integer: a whole number that can be positive, zero or negative.

irrational number: a number that is not a rational number and so cannot be represented as a decimal or as a fraction. Examples are $\sqrt{2}$ and π.

isosceles triangle: a triangle with two equal sides and two equal angles opposite to these sides.

kilometre: a unit of measure that equals 1,000 metres.

kite: a quadrilateral with adjacent sides equal to each other.

linear equation: an equation whose graph is a straight line.

line of symmetry: a line that divides a figure or shape into two equal parts.

mean: a method to find an average of a set of numbers, calculated by adding up all the numbers and dividing by the number of values.

mixed number: a whole number plus a proper fraction, e.g. $5\frac{3}{4}$.

mode: is the number that occurs most frequently in a set of numbers. For example with the set of numbers 2, 4, 4, 4, 5, 6, 6, 7, the number 4 is the mode.

multiples: the multiples of 10 are 10, 20, 30, 40, 50, and so on. Similarly the multiples of 4 are 4, 8, 12, 16, 20, 24, 28, . . .

natural number: the positive integers 1, 2, 3, 4, and so on.

negative integer: an integer less than zero.

net: a flat shape that can be folded to form a solid.

nonagon: a nine-sided polygon.

numeral: the symbol used to represent a number.

numerator: the top number of a fraction.

obtuse angle: an angle between 90° and 180°.

octagon: an eight-sided polygon.

ordinal number: a number that is a label on a number line. The concept of a number as a label for putting things in order.

parallelogram: a quadrilateral with opposite sides parallel and equal in length.

pentagon: a five-sided polygon.

perimeter: the total length around the edge of a shape.

place value: the position of a digit in a number determines its value. For example 4 can represent four, forty, four hundred and so on.

polygon: a 2D closed shape with straight sides, e.g. triangles, rectangles, pentagons, hexagons.

polyhedron: a 3D shape with only straight edges and plane surfaces.

positive integer: an integer greater than zero.

power: notation used to simplify and abbreviate calculations, e.g. $6 \times 6 \times 6 \times 6 = 6^4$.

prism: a polyhedron consisting of two opposite identical faces with their vertices joined by parallel sides.

product: the result of a multiplication. For example 12×9 gives a product of 108.

proper fraction: a fraction in which the numerator is smaller than the denominator, e.g. $\frac{3}{5}$.

pyramid: a polyhedron consisting of a polygon as a base, with straight lines drawn from each of the vertices of the base to meet at one point. This point where the lines meet is called the apex. Two common examples are the triangular and square based pyramids.

quadrilateral: a plane shape with four sides and four interior angles. These four interior angles add up to 360°.

quotient: the result when one number is divided by another number.

radius: a straight line from the centre of a circle to any point on the circumference of the circle. This length is half the diameter.

ratio: this is the relationship between two numbers of the same kind. For every amount of one, there is so much of another. For example 6 apples and 4 oranges can be expressed in the ratio 3:2.

rational number: a number that can be expressed as the ratio of two integers. All whole numbers and fractions are members of the group of rationals.

real number: any number that can be represented by a point on a number line. All the rational and irrational numbers are members of this set.

rectangle: a special parallelogram in which all four internal angles are 90°.

reflect angle: an angle between 180° and 360°.

regular polygon: a polygon in which all sides are equal in length and all the angles are equal in size.

remainder: this is the amount left when a division calculation does not result in a whole number. For example $21 \div 4 = 5$ remainder 1, which can be written as $5\frac{1}{4}$.

rhombus: a parallelogram in which all four sides are equal in length. Another name is an equilateral quadrilateral or a diamond.

scalene triangle: a triangle with all three sides of different lengths.

square: a special rectangle with all four sides equal in length.

square number: a number that can be obtained by multiplying a whole number by itself. For example 1, 4, 9, 16, 25, ...

translation: a transformation in which a shape is moved from one position to another without turning.

trapezium: a quadrilateral with two parallel sides.

vertex: is the corner point where the sides meet in a geometric shape with straight edges.

vulgar fraction: the same as a 'common fraction', in other words a fraction expressed as a numerator over a denominator, e.g. $\frac{3}{4}$.

References

Ainley, J., Bagnib, G. T., Hefendehl-Hebekerc, L. and Lagranged, J. B. (2009) Algebraic thinking and mathematics education. In *Proceeding of CERME*, 6 January, 28 February, 2009, Lyon, France pp. 415–419.

Askew, M., Rhodes, V., Brown, M., Williams, D. and Johnson, D. (1997) *Effective Teachers of Numeracy*. Report of a study carried out for the Teacher Training Agency by School of Education Kings College London.

Averbach, B. and Chein, O. (2000) *Problem Solving Through Recreational Mathematics*. Dover Publication, New York.

Ball, D. (1992) Magical hopes: manipulatives and the reform of math education. *American Educator*, Volume 16, No. 2, pp. 14–18 and pp. 46–47

Behrends, E. and Humble S. (2013) Triangle mysteries. *The Mathematical Intelligencer*, Volume 35, No. 2, pp. 10–15.

Budd, C. J. and Sangwin, C. J. (2001) *Mathematics Galore!* Oxford University Press, Oxford.

Cahill, L. and McGaugh, J. L. (1998) Mechanisms of emotional arousal and lasting declarative memory. *Trends in Neuroscience (TINS)*, Volume 21, No. 7, pp. 294–299

Dudeney, H. E. (1917) *Amusements in Mathematics*. Dover Publications, New York.

Eddy, E. (1969) *Becoming a Teacher: The Passage to Professional Status*. Teachers College Press, New York.

Euclid (1956) *The Thirteen Books of The Elements*. Dover Publications, New York.

Feynman, R. P. (2007) *What Do You Care What Other People Think?* Penguin Books, London.

Fulves, K. (1983) *Self-Working Number Magic: 101 Foolproof Tricks.* Dover Publications, New York.

Gardner, M. (1956) *Mathematics Magic and Mystery.* Dover Publications, New York.

Gattegno, C. (1971) *What We Owe Children: The Subordination of Teaching to Learning.* Routledge and Kegan Paul, London.

Hart, K., Johnstob, D., Brown, M., Dickson, L. and Clarkson, R. (1989) *Children's Mathematical Frameworks 8–13. A Study of Classroom Teaching.* Nottingham, Shell Centre for Mathematical Education.

Hofstadter, D. (1979) *Godel, Escher and Bach: An Eternal Golden Braid. A Metaphorical Fugue on Mind and Machines in the Spirit of Lewis Carroll.* Penguin Books, London.

Humble, S. (2002) *The Experimenters A to Z of Maths.* David Fulton Press, London.

Humble, S. (2012–2014) Dr Maths Puzzles Books: *Addition, Subtraction, Multiplication, Division, Fraction, Decimal, Time, Algebra Explorer, Code Breaker, Number Shape Magic.* High Wycombe, The Green Board Game Co.

Humble, S. (2013) *Maths for Every Day! 366 Primary Maths Activities Linked to Every Day of the Year.* TTS, Kirkby-in-Ashfield, Nottinghamshire.

Humble, S. (2013) *Playground Maths Activity Cards.* TTS, Kirkby-in-Ashfield, Nottinghamshire.

Kahneman, D. and Tversky. A. (1982) *Judgement under Uncertainty: Heuristics and Bias.* Cambridge University Press, New York.

McGaugh, J. L., Ferry, B. Vazdarjanova, A. and Roozendaal, B. (2000) Amygdala: role in modulation of memory storage. In *The Amygdala: A Functional Analysis* (Aggleton, J. P., ed.), pp. 391–423, Oxford University Press, London.

Mandelbrot, B. B. and Freeman, W. H. (1983) *The Fractal Geometry of Nature.* W.H. Freeman, San Francisco, CA.

Marland, M. (1975) *The Craft of the Classroom.* Heinemann Educational Books, Portsmouth, NH.

Munby, H. (1982) The place of teachers' beliefs in research on teacher thinking and decision making and an alternative methodology. *Instructional Science,* Volume 11, pp. 201–225.

Nespor, J. (1987) The role of beliefs in the practice of teaching. *Journal of Curriculum Studies*, Volume 19, pp. 317–328.

Ryan, J. and Williams, J. (2007) *Children's Mathematics 4–15: Learning from Errors and Misconceptions*. Open University Press, Maidenhead.

Scarne, J. (1950) *Scarne on Card Tricks*. Dover Publications, New York.

Schank, R. and Abelson, R. (1977) *Scripts, Plans, Goals and Understanding: An Inquiry into Human Knowledge Structures*. Lawrence Erlbaum, Hillsdale, NJ.

Schoenfeld, A. H. (2011) *How We Think: A Theory of Goal-Oriented Decision Making and its Educational Applications*. Routledge, Oxford.

Index

Al-Khwarizmi 94
Albers, Josef 70
Algorithm 94
Ali, Muhammad 36
Archimedes 38
art exhibition 69

Babylonians 18, 54
bar charts 84–85
breakfast 9, 60

calendar 54
Cassini oval 70
cauliflowers 6
Celsius scale 85–86
Chinese numbers 19, 38, 78–81, 114
chunking 48–49
Cuisenaire rods 38

da Vinci, Leonardo 38, 118
de Moivre, Abraham 81, 89
Dee, John 98–99
digital root 23–26
dinosaurs 56–57

eco-issues 87–88
Einstein, Albert 17, 21–22, 68
Egyptians 19, 54, 93; fractions 37–38

episodic learning 23, 111, 115
Escher, Maurits 74
Euclid 4–5, 67–68
Euler, Leonhard 68, 105–106

Fahrenheit, Daniel Gabriel 85–86
fractals 6, 72
fraction snap 40

Gauss, Carl Friedrich 33–34, 68, 81
Goldilocks and the Three Bears 87
Goldsworthy, Andy 70–71
Greeks 33, 38, 67–68, 93–94, 118
Greenwich Mean Time 54
golden ratio 38, 118

Halfway down the stairs 83–84
Hepburn, Audrey 22
hexiamonds 74, 76–77
human sundials 62-63

I Spy shape 72

Kepler, Johannes 69
Feynman, Richard 97
Klee, Paul 69–70

line graph 85

Mandelbrot, Benoit 6
Marland, Michael 23
maze 58
Milne, A. A. 83–84
mirror code 78
monsters 56–57

nets of shapes 73–74
non-standard units 54, 84
numerology 20–22

pictograms 85
pocket money 26–28
Platonic solids 68
prime numbers 31–32, 124
Pythagoras 19–21

Quayside maths walk 14

ratio 56–57, 118
repeated subtraction 49–50

robot 59
Romans 54, 126

scatter plots 85
St Swithun's Day 91
standard units 55
story 9, 21, 38, 56–59, 83, 87
supermarket 73, 114
symbol 34–35, 65, 94–95, 97–98

tally chart 15, 72
transfer triggers 12, 52, 84, 101,
    108, 113, 115
triangular numbers 33–34
tube station walk 15–16

Venn diagram 44–45
Visual representations 35;
    fractions 41–43

Walkers crisps 51–52

zombies 59